Lecture Notes in Computer Science   5844

Commenced Publication in 1973
Founding and Former Series Editors:
Gerhard Goos, Juris Hartmanis, and Jan van Leeuwen

T0223452

John C. Strassner
Yacine M. Ghamri-Doudane (Eds.)

Modelling Autonomic Communications Environments

Fourth IEEE International Workshop, MACE 2009
Venice, Italy, October 26-27, 2009
Proceedings

 Springer

Volume Editors

John C. Strassner
Pohang University of Science and Technology (POSTECH)
790-784 San 31, Hyoja-Dong, Nam-Gu, Pohang, Gyungbuk, Korea
E-mail: johns@postech.ac.kr

Yacine M. Ghamri-Doudane
Laboratoire d'informatique Gaspard-Monge - UMR CNRS 8049 (IGM-LabInfo)
77454 Marne-la-Vallée Cedex 2, France
and
Ecole Nationale Supérieure d'Informatique
pour l'industrie et l'entreprise (ENSIIE)
1 Square de la résistance, 91025 Evry cedex, France
E-mail: yacine.ghamri@ensiie.fr

Library of Congress Control Number: 2009936721

CR Subject Classification (1998): C.2, C.0, C.2.2, C.4, I.6, D.4.4, D.2

LNCS Sublibrary: SL 5 – Computer Communication Networks and
Telecommunications

ISSN   0302-9743
ISBN-10   3-642-05005-0 Springer Berlin Heidelberg New York
ISBN-13   978-3-642-05005-3 Springer Berlin Heidelberg New York

springer.com

© Springer-Verlag Berlin Heidelberg 2009
Printed in Germany

Typesetting: Camera-ready by author, data conversion by Scientific Publishing Services, Chennai, India
Printed on acid-free paper   SPIN: 12775859   06/3180   5 4 3 2 1 0

Preface

Research and development of autonomics have come a long way, and we are delighted to present the proceedings of the 4th IEEE International Workshop on Modeling Autonomic Communications Environments (MACE 2009). As in the last three years, this workshop was held as part of Manweek, the International Week on Management of Networks and Services, which took place in the culturally rich city of Venice in Italy. Manweek is now an umbrella of five workshops and conferences focusing on different aspects of network and service management, including MACE, distributed operations and management (DSOM), IP-based management (IPOM), towards multimedia and mobile networks (MMNS), and virtualization and middleware for next generation networks (NGNM). Further information of Manweek and the individual workshops and conferences can be found at http://www.manweek.org.

MACE started as an experiment, in 2006, and created a small community that now finds itself attracted back each year by a feeling of excitement and anticipation to share new advances and development. Certainly, MACE is not as shiny or practiced as other well-known conferences and workshops, but we consider this a feature of the workshop itself. New ideas, a little rough around the edges (and sometimes more than a little), often quite unfinished, pop out and provoke extensive discussion. Science needs this kind of exploratory adventure, and we have been strongly motivated to continue preserving this atmosphere of exploration and discussion in this year's technical program.

This year, the submissions were closely related to the main themes of the workshop. We saw new architectural designs as well as new applications of autonomic principles to specific networking problems. This depicts a maturity in the domain, which is entering a second round of research work taking advantages from the lessons learned in the last few years. We can call this part of MACE the "renewal of autonomics," acknowledging that we still have some way to go towards defining additional principles and fully establishing autonomic management as the standard for use.

We are very proud to present you this year's proceedings as a volume of Springer's *Lecture Notes in Computer Science* (LNCS) again. This book presents the accepted papers of the technical sessions of MACE 2009. We had, overall, 13 submissions, of which we accepted 6 as full papers. Furthermore, we allowed three submissions as short papers. Each paper was reviewed by at least three experts in the domain. Furthermore, to make sure that the accepted papers provided an interesting program, we discussed all submissions and all the reviews provided by the MACE TPC in full detail. We believe that, to support the objectives of MACE, this effort was well-worth doing and we hope that this book provides you with cutting-edge ideas, thoughtful presented solutions and pursuable experiments.

Finally, we would like to thank the many people whose hard work and commitment were essential to the success of MACE 2009. Foremost amongst these are the researchers who submitted papers to the workshop. We would like to express our gratitude to the MACE Technical Program Committee for their advice and support through all the stages of the workshop preparation. We thank all reviewers for their fair and helpful reviews. We thank the IEEE Communications Society and the Autonomic Communications Forum (AFC) for support and sponsorship of MACE. Most of the more time-consuming practical and logistical organization tasks for the workshop were handled by the members of the Manweek 2009 Organizing Committee – this made our jobs significantly easier, and for that we are very grateful. Finally, we wish to acknowledge the financial support of the Manweek sponsors, whose contributions were hugely instrumental in helping us run what we hope was a stimulating, rewarding and, most importantly, an enjoyable workshop for all its participants.

October 2009   John Strassner
                                                                   Yacine Ghamri-Doudane

MACE 2009 Organization

Conference and Program Co-chairs

John Strassner   POSTECH, Korea
Yacine Ghamri-Doudane   IGM-LabInfo & ENSIIE, France

Steering Committee

John Strassner   POSTECH, Korea
Nazim Agoulmine   University of Evry, France
Sven van der Meer   TSSG, Ireland
Joel Fleck   HP, USA
Brendan Jennings   TSSG, Ireland

Publication Advisory Chair

Tom Pfeifer   Waterford Institute of Technology, Ireland

Publication Chair

Alberto Gonzalez Prieto   Royal Institute of Technology (KTH), Sweden

Finance Chair

Raouf Boutaba   University of Waterloo, Canada

Infrastructure Chair

Sven van der Meer   Waterford Institute of Technology, Ireland

Local Arrangements Chair

Massimo Foscato   Telecom Italia Labs, Italy

Registration Chair

Idilio Drago   University of Twente, The Netherlands

Publicity Co-chair

Carlos Becker Westphall   Federal University of Santa Catarina (UFSC),
                               Brazil

Manweek 2009 General Co-chairs

Aiko Pras   University of Twente, The Netherlands
Roberto Saracco   Telecom Italia Labs, Italy

Manweek 2009 Advisors

Raouf Boutaba   University of Waterloo, Canada
James Hong   POSTECH, Korea
Aiko Pras   University of Twente, The Netherlands

MACE 2009 Technical Program Committee

Abdelhakim Hafid   University of Montreal, Canada
Abdelmalek Benzekri   Université Paul Sabatier, France
Ahmed Karmouch   University of Ottawa, Canada
David Lewis   Trinity College Dublin, Ireland
Declan O'Sullivan   Trinity College Dublin, Ireland
Dominique Dudkowski   NEC, Germany
Edmundo Madeira   UNICAMP, Brazil
Falko Dressler   University of Erlangen, Germany
Filip De Turck   Ghent University, IBBT, Belgium
Francine Krief   LaBRI Laboratory, Bordeaux 1 University,
                               France
Georg Carle   Technical University of Munich, Germany
James Hong   POSTECH, Korea
Joan Serrat   Universitat Politècnica de Catalunya, Spain
Joaquim Celestino Júnior   State university of Cear, UECE, Brazil
José De Souza   UFC, Brazil
Jose-Marcos Nogueira   UFMG, Brazil
Karima Boudaoud   I3S-CNRS Laboratory, University of Nice
                               Sophia Antipolis, Brazil
Laurent Ciavaglia   Alcatel-Lucent, France
Lisandro Zambenedetti
Granville   UFRGS, Brazil
Lozano José   Telefónica Investigacin y Desarrollo, Spain
Martin Huddleston   QinetiQ Limited, UK
Maurice Mulvenna   University of Ulster, UK
Mieso Denko   Univeristy of Guelph, Canada

Peter Deussen	Fraunhofer Institute for Open Communication Systems, Germany
Simon Dobson	University College Dublin, Ireland
Spyros Denazis	Hitachi Europe & University of Patras, Greece
Tadashi Nakano	University of California, Irvine, USA

Additional Reviewers

Clarissa Marquezan	UFRGS, Brazil
Gerhard Münz	TU München, Germany
Ibrahim Aloqily	Hashemite University, Jordan
Neumar Malheiros	UNICAMP, Brazil
Stenio Fernandes	University of Ottawa / IF-AL, Canada
Tim Wauters	University of Ghent, Belgium

Table of Contents

Invited Paper

Session A – Theory of Autonomic Management

Session B – Applying Autonomic Principles

Session C – Short Papers

Combining Learned and Highly-Reactive Management

Alva L. Couch and Marc Chiarini

Computer Science Department
Tufts University
Medford, MA, USA
couch@cs.tufts.edu, marc.chiarini@tufts.edu

Abstract. Learned models of behavior have the disadvantage that they must be retrained after any change in system configuration. Autonomic management methods based upon learned models lose effectiveness during the retraining period. We propose a hybrid approach to autonomic resource management that combines management based upon learned models with "highly-reactive" management that does not depend upon learning, history, or complete information. Whenever re-training is necessary, a highly-reactive algorithm serves as a fallback management strategy. This approach mitigates the risks involved in using learned models in the presence of unpredictable effects, including unplanned configuration changes and hidden influences upon performance not considered in the learned model. We use simulation to demonstrate the utility of the hybrid approach in mitigating pitfalls of both learning-based and highly-reactive approaches.

Keywords: autonomic computing, convergent operators, computer immunology, self-organizing systems, emergent properties, Cfengine.

1 Introduction

In the literature, the term "autonomic computing" seems to have become synonymous with employing control loops to control a closed system[1,2,3]. In this paper, we propose an alternate approach to autonomic resource management based upon an *open-world assumption* that at least some influences upon the managed system are not just unknown, but also *unobservable*, *unlearnable*, and *unknowable*. While open-world systems may perchance behave like closed-loop systems, such behavior is not guaranteed, and at any time, open-world behavior may arise.

An open-world assumption is necessary in order to manage many kinds of contemporary computing systems, e.g., virtual instances of servers in clouds. By design, a cloud server instance is not supposed to know about co-location of other services on the same physical server, but such co-location can and does influence performance as a *hidden variable*. Thus any management strategy for optimizing the behavior of cloud server instances must presume the existence of *unobservable influences* upon the managed system.

J.C. Strassner and Y.M. Ghamri-Doudane (Eds.): MACE 2009, LNCS 5844, pp. 1–14, 2009.

1.1 Immunology and Approximation

We cope with unobservable influences partly by adopting Burgess' immunological approach to autonomic control[4]. In the immunological approach, management is expressed as voluntary cooperation between an ensemble of independently-acting distributed agents; the result of management is an emergent property of that ensemble. This is the philosophy behind the management tool Cfengine[5,6], which provides one kind of management agent. Burgess demonstrated that the Cfengine paradigm is guaranteed to converge to predictable states[4,7] and is perhaps best characterized as accomplishing management by seeking states of "thermodynamic equilibrium"[8,9], where that equilibrium is an emergent property[10,11] of the system and agents. Burgess and Couch demonstrated that autonomic computing can be "approximated" by the Cfengine paradigm[12]. The decentralized nature of the Cfengine paradigm is perhaps best described using the concept of a *promise*[13,14]: a non-binding statement of intent from one agent to another. The input to a Cfengine agent is a set of promises, while its output is a sequence of actions intended to seek equilibrium and thus put the system into a desirable state.

We began this work by seeking an appropriate solution for the problem of autonomic resource management via use of Burgess' autonomous agents. Resource management refers to the problem of matching resource availability for a computation to the performance demands for the computation. For example, in an elastic cloud, one must match the number of available servers for an application with the demand for that application; if there is low demand, one server might suffice, while a high-demand situation might require hundreds of servers. While theoretical results implied that resource management is possible via autonomous agents, no solution was obvious from the theory.

We thus sought a formulation of resource management compatible with Burgess' autonomic computing model. This paper is the third in a series on this topic.

1.2 Closures and Cost-Value Tradeoffs

In the first paper[15] in the series, we developed the idea of a resource closure and the basics of open-world resource management. A closure is a predictable (and thus closed) subsystem of an otherwise open system[16,17,18,19]. We proposed a resource management paradigm based upon two kinds of agents: a *resource closure agent* that manages the resource, and several *gatekeeper agents* that provide performance feedback to the resource closure. The closure makes resource allocation decisions based upon a *cost-value tradeoff*; the closure knows the *cost* C of resources, while the gatekeepers know the *value* V of performance. Thus the closure attempts to *maximize reward,* which is the difference between value and cost $(V - C)$. In the following, we will refer to $V - C$ as the *objective function* to be maximized. We demonstrated that $V - C$ can be managed to near-optimal levels by simple hill-climbing *without* knowledge of the (perhaps hidden) performance influences, provided that there are sufficient constraints on the behavior of those influences and the nature of V and C as functions. If those constraints are violated, even catastrophically, the system still converges eventually to a stable, near-optimal state, which stays near-optimal as long as constraints (on hidden variables) continue to be satisfied. Thus the hill-climbing approach is *highly reactive* in the sense that it can react to unforeseen changes efficiently and without an appreciable learning curve.

The key result of the first paper is that *one can trade constraints for model precision* in managing a complex system; constraints on the managed system are as important as model precision in achieving management objectives. Management can meet objectives even if the model does not account for any performance influences at all; hill-climbing still meets management objectives as long as hidden influences obey reasonable constraints. Even if constraints are not met, hill-climbing continues to eventually meet management objectives, although the response time is slower than desired.

1.3   Step-Function SLAs and Level Curve Analysis

One weakness of the approach in the first paper is that hill-climbing requires that value V and cost C are simply increasing functions that are never constant on an interval. In realistic cases, cost and value are both step functions: one cannot (usually) allocate part of a server as a resource, while Service-Level Agreements (SLAs) specify value as a step-function depending upon performance.

In the second paper of this series[20], we discussed how to handle step functions for cost C and value V. Value V is a function $V(P)$ of system performance P, while cost C is a function $C(R)$ of resources R. While closed-world management relates performance P and resources R via some (assumed or learned) model of behavior, in an open-world system, performance P and resources R are *incommensurate*, in the sense that no fixed model relates the two concepts to one another. Thus the problem of choosing R to maximize $V(P) - C(R)$ requires first relating P and R in some meaningful way, so that one can estimate value $V(R)$ and cost $C(R)$ both as functions of the same independent variable R.

As time progresses, costs C are fixed while performance P varies with time-varying hidden influences. Thus the step function $V(R) \approx V(P(R))$ varies with time. While the range of V is fixed by the SLA, the resource levels R at which $V(R)$ changes in value vary over time and are predicted by a model of $P(R)$.

Step-functions expose a weakness in the incremental strategy. Incremental hill-climbing – which serves us well when value and cost functions have no steps – now leads to situations in which the incremental search spends too much time with sub-optimal reward. Increments to resources during hill-climbing are too small to keep up with drastic step-changes in $V - C$.

1.4   A Hybrid Approach

In this paper, we take the final step in proposing an immunological approach to resource management. We combine highly-reactive hill-climbing with simple machine learning to exploit the strengths of both approaches. We first describe the control architecture and the hybrid model by which we accomplish control. We simulate the model in simple cases to compare behaviors of the hybrid model to behaviors of its components. Our conclusions include limitations of the hybrid approach, as well as a discussion of remaining challenges in open-world resource management.

2   Our Control Architecture

Our basic control architecture is depicted in Figure 1. A managed system M is controlled through a vector of resource parameters R and influenced by a known load L and unknown factors X. A gatekeeper (e.g., a load balancer) G observes L and system performance P in response to L. G knows the resources R utilized by the managed system. G also knows the value function $V(P)$ of performance P (as specified by an SLA). G uses the history of observed triples (P, R, L) that it observes over time to estimate $P(R, L)$ and thus, to estimate $V(R, L) \approx V(P(R, L))$. Holding L constant at its current value, G communicates

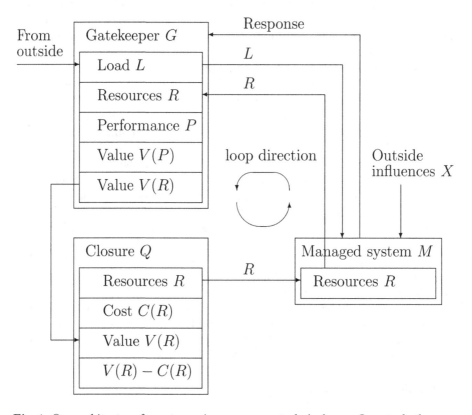

Fig. 1. Our architecture for autonomic resource control. A closure Q controls the managed system M, whose performance P is observed by the gatekeeper G, which informs Q of an observed value function V, thus closing the control loop.

an estimate of $V(R)$ to the closure Q. Q combines that estimate with its own knowledge of $C(R)$ to obtain an estimate of the objective function $V(P(R)) - C(R)$. Q uses this estimate to choose the next value for R, thus closing the control loop. $P(R, L)$ is assumed to be simply increasing in R and simply decreasing in L. $C(R)$ and $V(P)$ are assumed to be increasing step functions in R and P, respectively.

In this paper, the notation $P(R, L)$ refers to a hypothetical functional dependency between P and V; likewise writing $V(P(R, L))$ refers to a hypothetical functional dependency between (R, L) and P, and between P and V. The statement $V(R, L) \approx V(P(R, L))$ means that there is a (hypothetical) functional dependency between (R, L) and V that is a (transitive) result of the (hypothetical) functional dependencies between (R, L) and P, and between P and V. Sometimes, these functional relationships are known for sure, e.g., $V(P)$ or $C(R)$; sometimes they must be estimated, e.g., $P(R, L)$.

This is an *open control loop*, because G and Q have no knowledge whatever of the managed system's input X that might influence P. In theory, $P = P(R, L, X)$, and not $P(R, L)$; estimates $P(R, L)$ do not account for the hidden (and unobservable) variable X, so that the estimates of $V(P(R, L))$ likewise do not account for X. The ideal of observing X and estimating $P(R, L, X)$ and $V(P(R, L, X))$ is considered to be impossible; X represents the *unobservable* and *unknowable* component of influences upon M.

For example, consider a cloud computing environment. M represents the cloud infrastructure, while G represents a load balancer at the border and Q represents the elasticity manager. G can measure the performance of instances, but does not have knowledge of external influences X such as co-location of other services with the current services (on the same physical server). G cannot obtain such information without agreements with other clients of the cloud; such information is *unobservable* and thus *unknowable*.

This architecture differs from those we studied previously in one important aspect: we allow G to utilize knowledge of L in modeling $P(R, L)$; in previous work, G modeled only $P(R)$ and did not utilize L. Adding L to the model allows the new architecture to intelligently deal with step-functions for cost and value. As in prior work, however, X remains as an unknowable load parameter.

3   Two Approaches to Control

The controller Q in the proposed architecture utilizes a hybrid control strategy incorporating two kinds of control:

1. *Reactive* control based upon localized state and behavior.
2. *Learned* control based upon accumulated history of behavior.

Reactive control incrementally changes R in a small neighborhood of the current R setting, based upon observations and predictions that are local to the current system state in both time and space. This control mechanism makes mistakes due to lack of knowledge of X, but quickly corrects those mistakes via aggressive experimentation[15]. It reacts slowly, however, to major situational changes requiring large swings in R settings, and fails to determine optimal behavior if the objective function $V - C$ is not convex, i.e., if it has more than one local maximum that is not a global maximum.

Learned control changes R according to some learned model of $P(R, L)$ based upon a long-term history. Learned control bases new R values upon *global* prediction of future state. It reacts quickly to changes in observable requirements, e.g., rapid swings in L, but slowly to changes in hidden factors or system architecture, e.g., replacements of system components that invalidate collected history. Thus learned control is invalidated when current behavior becomes dissimilar to historical data.

These control paradigms are in some sense opposites. Prior work demonstrated that reactive control has an opposite character to that of machine learning[15]: incorporating more history into reactive control *increases* reaction time to mistakes as well as recovery and convergence time.

4   Selecting a Control Mechanism

Our open-world assumption means that no learned model can ever be considered definitive. Instead, we propose a hybrid architecture in which learned control and highly-reactive control are chosen depending upon conditions. The key to our hybrid strategy is to choose a mechanism by which the validity of the learned model can be tested. If the learned model tests as valid, then learned control is used, while if the learned model fails the validity test, the reactive model is utilized instead.

After testing several validity measures, we settled upon studying the simplest one: a statistical measure commonly referred to as the "coefficient of determination" or r^2[1]. If $\{X_i\}$ is a set of samples, $\hat{X}_i$ represents the prediction for X_i, and $\overline{X}$ represents the mean of $\{X_i\}$, then the coefficient of determination is

$$r^2 = 1 - (\Sigma(X_i - \hat{X}_i)^2))/\Sigma(X_i - \overline{X})^2$$

r^2 is a unitless quantity that varies between 0 and 1; it is 1 if the model exactly predicts behavior, and 0 if the model is useless in predicting behavior. In our case, the history consists of triples (P_i, R_i, L_i) , and the coefficient of determination for the model P is:

$$r^2 = 1 - (\Sigma(P(R_i, L_i) - P_i)^2)/(\Sigma(P_i - \overline{P})^2)$$

where $\overline{P}$ is the mean of the $\{P_i\}$, and $P(R_i, L_i)$ represents the specific model prediction of P_i from R_i and L_i.

Use of the coefficient of determination to test goodness-of-fit is a subtle choice, and not equivalent to using goodness-of-fit tests for the model itself. Our goodness-of-fit test is intentionally *less powerful* than those utilized in model fitting, but also *more general* in the sense that it is independent of the way in which the model was constructed. It can thus be used to compare models constructed in different ways, even with offline models not fitted to the current history.

---

[1] The name "r^2" is traditional in statistics and has no relationship to our R, which is a measure of resources.

5   Simulations

Our proposed control system has many variables, and a quantitative study would require specifying too many details. For this paper, we will instead simulate and remark upon the qualitative behavior of the system when exposed to various kinds of events.

We simulate the simplest possible system amenable to the two kinds of control. Our system obeys the linear response law

$$P = \alpha R/(L + X) + \beta + \epsilon(0, \sigma)$$

where α and β are constants, and ϵ represents a normally-distributed measurement error function with mean 0 and standard deviation σ. Recall that the gatekeeper G cannot measure or observe X. Learned control is thus achieved by determining constant coefficients α and β such that

$$P(R, L) \approx \alpha R/L + \beta$$

through linear least-squares estimation. We can then maximize

$$V(P) - C(R) \approx V(\alpha R/L + \beta) - C(R)$$

by choosing an appropriate R. If the r^2 statistic for $P(R, X)$ is sufficiently near to 1.0 (e.g., ≥ 0.9) then this estimate of R is used (the learning strategy); otherwise, a short-term model of P is utilized to estimate local benefit from changing R incrementally (the reactive strategy).

5.1   Simulator Details

We experimented with the proposed algorithm using a simulator written in the R statistics system[21]. Although there are now many ways to estimate the response of a managed system via machine learning, several qualitative properties of our proposed architecture arise from even the simplest systems. We simulate the response of a simple system, employing statistical learning, to various kinds of events. The system's (hidden) response function is

$$P(R, L, X) = 1.0 * R/(L + X) + 0.0$$

This is not known to the simulated gatekeeper G, which instead estimates α and β according to:

$$P(R, L) \approx \alpha R/L + \beta$$

by linear least-squares estimation. The learned strategy utilizes 200 time steps of history to estimate P, while the reactive strategy utilizes 10 time steps of history and the same model.

The value function $V(P)$ is known to G while the cost function $C(R)$ is known to Q. The value $V(P)$ is given by:

$$V(P) = \begin{cases} 0 \text{ if } P < 100 \\ 200 \text{ if } 100 \leq P < 175 \\ 400 \text{ if } 175 \leq P \end{cases}$$

while the cost $C(R)$ is given by:

$$C(R) = \begin{cases} 0 \text{ if } R < 100 \\ 100 \text{ if } 100 \leq R < 200 \\ 300 \text{ if } 200 \leq R \end{cases}$$

These functions are arbitrary and were chosen mainly because they have interesting properties, e.g., there is more than one optimal range for R.

Both learned and reactive strategies attempt to maximize $V(P) - C(R)$ by changing R. In the learned strategy, R is set to the recommended value, while in the reactive strategy, R is incremented toward the recommended value by 5 resource units at a time[2]. Using increments rather than settings compensates for errors that inevitably arise from the small number of samples utilized to estimate R in the reactive strategy.

Additionally, regardless of whether learned or reactive strategy is used, the R value is left alone if the current value of R is predicted to be optimal. If R is predicted to be optimal and does not change for 10 steps, it is incremented or decremented temporarily to explore whether the situation has changed, and then returned to its prior (optimal) value if no change is detected. This exploration is necessary to inform the reactive strategy of changes in situation.

In all simulations, Load L varies sinusoidally between 0.5 and 1.5 every 500 time steps. This leads to sinusoidal variation in the cutoffs for optimal $V - C$. Initially, measurement noise σ and unknown load X are set to 0. Each simulation consists of 1500 time steps, of which the first 500 steps of settling time are omitted from the figures.

In the following experimental results, plots consist of several layers as depicted in Figure 2. Acceptable goodness of fit is depicted as a light-gray background (upper left) when the goodness of fit measure r^2 (depicted as a curve) is greater than 0.9. When the background is light gray, learned management is being used; a white background means that reactive management is being used. The regions for R that theoretically maximize $V - C$ are depicted in dark gray (upper right); these always occur between horizontal lines representing where C changes and wavy lines representing where V changes; these are not known to G and G must estimate them. The trajectory of R over time (either recommended or observed) is depicted as a series of black dots (lower left). The composite plot shows the relationships between all four components (lower right).

5.2   Effects of Uncertainty

The combined strategy – not surprisingly – does relatively well at handling situations where there are no outside influences or small changes. However, there were some small surprises during simulation. Even a constant hidden influence $X = 0.5$ (50% of the average value of L) poses difficulties for the learned strategy(Figure 3) and the reactive strategy must compensate. In Figure 3, the upper left plot depicts

---

[2] In prior work we demonstrated that the size of this increment is a critical parameter[15]. In this work we size it near to optimality and leave the increment constant, because we are studying instead how to combine the two strategies.

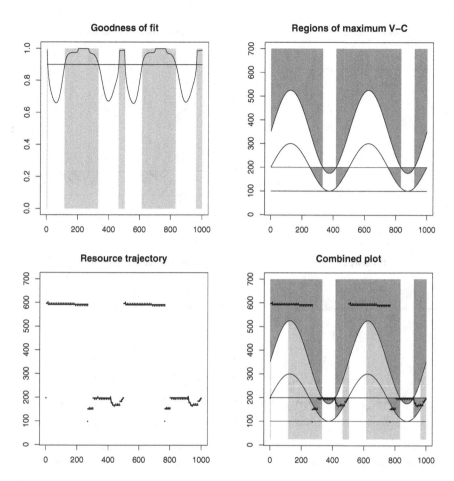

Fig. 2. We depict behavior of the combined strategy via plots that overlay goodness of fit (top left), maximum reward regions(top right), and actual resource trajectories(bottom left) into a single plot (bottom right). All horizontal axes represent time. The vertical axis of the top left plot is the coefficient of determination r^2, while the vertical axes of the other plots depict R.

goodness of fit, while the upper and lower right plots show the recommendations of the learned and reactive strategies. When the background becomes white, the reactive model is being used instead of the learned model. The lower left plot shows the actual management response of the system; this is also the plot whose construction is described in Figure 2. The goodness-of-fit varies with the magnitude of L, in rough proportion to the ratio of signal L to (hidden) noise X.

The behavior in Figure 3 is surprisingly similar to what happens when noise is injected into the measurements of L.[3] Again, goodness-of-fit varies with the magnitude of L and its relative magnitude to the magnitude of the noise.

---

[3] Results are omitted for brevity.

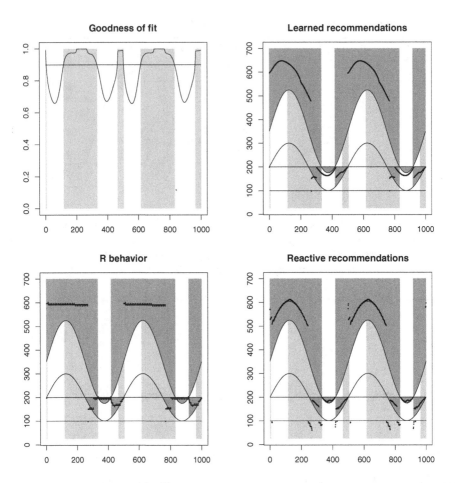

Fig. 3. Even a constant hidden load factor X, where X is $1/2$ of the average value of L, periodically invalidates predictions of the learned model (top right, white background) when the hidden influence becomes commensurate with known ones. During this time, predictions of the reactive model (bottom right, white background) control R, resulting in an actual R trajectory depicted on bottom left.

6   Dealing with Discontinuities

The two management strategies differ greatly in how they deal with discontinuities. A *discontinuity* is a relatively large change in some attribute of computation, e.g., load, hidden influences, policy, or model factors.

Discontinuities in input and discontinuous changes in objective function are no problem for a learned model; the model suggests a jump to an optimal resource level because the model is not compromised by the discontinuity. Discontinuities in the model itself (or – equivalently – discontinuities in hidden variables not accounted for by the model) are handled poorly by a learned model (whose accuracy is compromised) and handled better by a reactive strategy.

By contrast, reactive management deals well with situations of model flux but cannot easily cope with discontinuities in the input, such as sudden bursts of load. There is no model; therefore, there is nothing to invalidate in situations of great flux. But the exact same pattern of controlled, cautious experimentation that compensates for errors in judgement also makes it difficult for reactive management to deal with sudden, large changes in *input* and large discontinuities in the objective $(V - C)$ function.

An extreme form of model discontinuity is shown in Figure 4. At time $t = 500$, the underlying performance model changes from $P = 1R/(L + X) + 0$ to $P = 2R/(L + X) + 3$, simulating the complete and unexpected replacement of the server with one that is roughly twice as fast. The learned model is temporarily invalidated (and predicts resource values in the white region (upper right plot)),

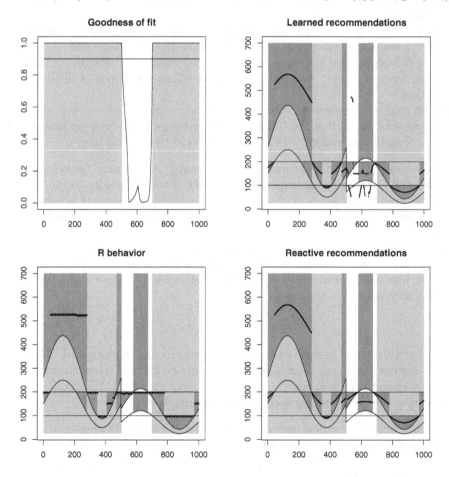

Fig. 4. Discontinuities in P invalidate the learned model (in the region with a white background) and require reactive help

and the reactive model takes over (lower left plot) and predicts near-optimal values of R until the learned model can discover what to do in the new situation. Other forms of model discontinuity behave similarly.

7   Conclusions

In designing this management approach, we utilized several unusual techniques, including:

1. *Trading accuracy of the model for constraints on changes in input.* The reactive strategy works well when changes are small, and requires no model accuracy to work properly.
2. *Exploiting opportunistic accuracy.* The learned strategy is useful even if it does not apply at all times, or even if its model oscillates between validity and invalidity.
3. *Compensating for inaccuracy via use of local data.* The reactive strategy avoids a learning curve by using only data from the immediate past.
4. *Using models to cope with input and objective function discontinuities.* The model, when accurate, can deal with sudden changes in input or objective function.
5. *Using local exploration to cope with hidden variables and sudden model changes and discontinuities.* The reactive strategy deals well with small changes and is not subject to validation limits of the learned model.

Several generalizations are relatively straightforward. Asynchrony between actions of G and Q, as well as multiple G's for one Q, is easy to handle and simply slows down response time. L, R, X, and P can be multi-dimensional as long as $P(L, R)$ remains linear and V and C remain single-dimensional step-functions of P and R.

But the door is closed permanently on several options previously believed to be potentially useful. Inferring an unobservable X in this situation turned out to be not just impractical, but impossible; brief experiments with non-linear regression to predict γ in the model

$$P \approx \alpha R/(L + \gamma) + \beta$$

showed that this model has too much freedom and γ is underdetermined. Using gradient-descent non-linear regression, γ could only be inferred when the initial γ was very close to the real one.

Simulating the algorithm exposed many new quandaries.

1. A significant but constant unknown parameter (X) is just as problematic to the validity of the learned model as is significant noise in the input (σ). X does not even have to vary to be problematic. The resulting behaviors seem to be indistinguishable.

2. All kinds of model discontinuity (e.g., changes in X and P) look similar from the point of view of the simulation. There is a recovery time in which the learned model learns the new situation while the incremental model handles management. During this recovery period, the incremental model deals poorly with further discontinuities in either input or model.

Several open questions remain:

1. Can we improve the behavior of the incremental algorithm during long learning periods?
2. Should several learned models with different learning times be utilized?
3. Can static models (e.g., offline learning) be utilized effectively via this mechanism?
4. Can we analyze the transient response of a composite system?

We believe that the answers to all of these questions are "yes", but only further work will tell.

The problem of open-world management is a difficult one, and we have only scratched the surface of the problem. The real underlying issue is one of human expectation. An open world precludes exact guarantees of management behavior. We can only estimate and bound behavior of such systems, and traditional control theory – with its dependence upon exact models – proves less than useful. Worse, in such a system, there is no way to know best-case behavior.

Ours is a story of complexity made simpler. Bounding behavior reduces the complexity of management processes, and dealing with cost and value (rather than more abstract ideas like "performance") simplifies the description of the management problem. A collection of simple management strategies – applied opportunistically – works better than a single strategy. Absolute precision is a thing of the past, and even the most imprecise strategies can contribute positively when things go wrong. This is a fairly good description of human management, as well as that accomplished by autonomic tools.

References

1. Hellerstein, J.L., Diao, Y., Parekh, S., Tilbury, D.M.: Feedback Control of Computing Systems. John Wiley & Sons, Chichester (2004)
2. Horn, P.: Autonomic computing: Ibm's perspective on the state of information technology (October 2001),
   http://researchweb.watson.ibm.com/autonomic/manifesto/
   autonomic_computing.pdf (cited April 16, 2009)
3. IBM: An architectural blueprint for autonomic computing (June 2006),
   http://www-01.ibm.com/software/tivoli/autonomic/pdfs/
   AC_Blueprint_White_Paper_4th.pdf (cited April 16, 2009)
4. Burgess, M.: Computer immunology. In: Proceedings of the Twelth Systems Administration Conference (LISA XII), p. 283. USENIX Association, Berkeley (1998)
5. Burgess, M.: Configurable immunity for evolving human-computer systems. Science of Computer Programming 51, 197 (2004)

6. Burgess, M.: A site configuration engine. Computing Systems 8(2), 309–337 (1995)
7. Burgess, M.: On the theory of system administration. Science of Computer Programming 49, 1 (2003)
8. Burgess, M.: Thermal, non-equilibrium phase space for networked computers. Physical Review E 62, 1738 (2000)
9. Burgess, M.: Keynote: The promise of self-adapting equilibrium. In: Proceedings of the Fifth IEEE International Conference on Autonomic Computing (ICAC) (June 2008)
10. Holland, J.H.: Emergence: From Chaos to Order. Oxford Univ. Pr. (Sd), Oxford (2000)
11. Johnson, S.: Emergence: The Connected Lives of Ants, Brains, Cities, and Software. Scribner (September 2002)
12. Burgess, M., Couch, A.: Autonomic computing approximated by fixed-point promises. In: Proceedings of the First IEEE International Workshop on Modeling Autonomic Communication Environments (MACE), pp. 197–222. Multicon Verlag (2006)
13. Burgess, M.: An approach to understanding policy based on autonomy and voluntary cooperation. In: Schönwälder, J., Serrat, J. (eds.) DSOM 2005. LNCS, vol. 3775, pp. 97–108. Springer, Heidelberg (2005)
14. Bergstra, J., Burgess, M.: A static theory of promises. Technical report, arXiv:0810.3294v1 (2008)
15. Couch, A.L., Chiarini, M.: Dynamics of resource closure operators. In: Sadre, R., Pras, A. (eds.) AIMS 2009. LNCS, vol. 5637, pp. 28–41. Springer, Heidelberg (2009)
16. Couch, A., Hart, J., Idhaw, E.G., Kallas, D.: Seeking closure in an open world: A behavioral agent approach to configuration management. In: LISA 2003: Proceedings of the 17th USENIX conference on System administration, pp. 125–148. USENIX, Berkeley (2003)
17. Schwartzberg, S., Couch, A.: Experience implementing a web service closure. In: LISA 2004: Proceedings of the 18th USENIX conference on System administration, pp. 213–230. USENIX, Berkeley (2004)
18. Wu, N., Couch, A.: Experience implementing an ip address closure. In: LISA 2006: Proceedings of the 20th USENIX conference on System administration, pp. 119–130. USENIX, Berkeley (2006)
19. Couch, A.L., Chiarini, M.: A theory of closure operators. In: Hausheer, D., Schönwälder, J. (eds.) AIMS 2008. LNCS, vol. 5127, pp. 162–174. Springer, Heidelberg (2008)
20. Couch, A.L., Burgess, M., Chiarini, M.: Management without (detailed) models. In: González Nieto, J., et al. (eds.) ATC 2009. LNCS, vol. 5586, pp. 75–89. Springer, Heidelberg (2009)
21. R Development Core Team: R: A Language and Environment for Statistical Computing. In: R Foundation for Statistical Computing, Vienna, Austria (2008) ISBN 3-900051-07-0

The Applicability of Self-Awareness for Network Management Operations

John Strassner[1,2], Sven van der Meer[2], and James Won-Ki Hong[1]

[1] Pohang University of Science and Technology (POSTECH), Pohang, Korea
{johns,jwkhong}@postech.ac.kr
[2] Telecommunications Systems & Software Group, Waterford Institute of Technology,
Ireland
{jstrassner,vdmeer}@tssg.org

Abstract. Network management operation will get increasingly more difficult in next generation and Future Internet scenarios due to many factors, such as mobility and the need for context-awareness. This position paper argues that the increasing complexity in business, system, and other operations can only be managed by making the systems aware of their own operations. This is shown by describing how *self-awareness* is implemented in the FOCALE autonomic architecture.

Keywords: Autonomic Architecture, Context, Context-Awareness, FOCALE, Management, Self-Awareness.

1 Introduction

The current success of the Internet architecture has spurred advances in business, social, and technical communications. However, that simplicity is also the source of many of its inherent limitations [1][2][3]. Two of the most important are its architectural limitations and its inability to relate business needs to network services and resources offered.

Most research communities ignore the management aspects of the Future Internet. One of the most fundamental of these aspects is the representation of management and operational data. Currently, such data has been built by network device manufacturers to ease the management of their (vendor-specific) device or device families. The vast majority of languages and data structures used by network device manufacturers, such as SNMP-based designs [4] and Command Line Interfaces [5], are *data-oriented* and are not conducive to representing *semantic* knowledge, such as the effects of a command, its hardware and/or software requirements, and the true *meaning* of what that command does. Furthermore, such languages have no ability to represent business concepts, such as a Service Level Agreement, or higher-level concepts, such as "maximize revenue for all users".

We believe that this can only be corrected by building a new representation of operational and management data. This position paper starts this process by examining the most fundamental characteristic of autonomic systems: *self-awareness*.

J.C. Strassner and Y.M. Ghamri-Doudane (Eds.): MACE 2009, LNCS 5844, pp. 15–28, 2009.

The organization of the rest of this paper is as follows. Section 2 defines self-awareness, and analyzes its implications for network management. Sections 3 and 4 describe how self-awareness is represented and implemented in FOCALE, while Section 5 provides conclusions and describes our future work.

2 Self-Awareness for Network Management

This section first provides a definition of self-awareness. Then, an overview of the problems caused by a lack of self-awareness for networks and network-based applications are provided. This is followed by an analysis of related work.

2.1 Definition of Self-Awareness

The definition of self-awareness has its roots in philosophy and psychology, where the concept of "self" is defined as the explicit consciousness an entity has regarding its own existence, often realized as its own distinct identity, and the general notion of well-being (e.g., knowing how to defend itself from predators) [6]. This usually includes a realization that the entity is distinct from other entities. In theory, autonomic systems should extend this notion of "self" to non-human things [7][8]. In [8], this is done by distinguishing between self-aware, or autonomous, entities and non-self-aware, or allonomous, entities, based on the observation that the former can govern their own actions, while the latter cannot. In fact, the latter have *limited* governance capabilities, since they have to rely on external control.

Since non-living entities do not have a notion of "consciousness", self-awareness must instead be viewed as a *cognitive* characteristic. The point of self-awareness is *not* to be able to create an arbitrary artificial intelligence without any goals. Rather, the use of self-awareness is to decrease the complexity of managing and using components and systems. In the FOCALE [9] autonomic architecture, the system can support a set of goals that are not limited to maintaining a single state, but instead have the ability to choose the desired *resulting* state from among a set of acceptable system states [8]. This gives the system the freedom to utilize its inherent intelligence to adjust the actions it takes in response to changing user needs, environmental conditions, or business goals. This approach solves difficult problems such as "maximize revenue from all users" by using a combination of utility functions with goal- and event-condition-action policies to reconfigure the network according to the needs of the business. The translation between network and business terms is explained in [27].

We define *self-awareness* in FOCALE as the ability of an entity to understand its own behavior as well as that desired of it. This latter includes modeling applicable business rules as well as environmental conditions. The behavior of an entity can thus be related to attaining one or more goals in a specific context; those goals may be defined by the entity and/or given to the entity as directives from an external source. This implies that in order to be self-aware, the entity must be able to (1) understand the significance of any constraints against achieving those goals, and (2) either directly or indirectly monitor its progress in achieving its goals, and at any time deduce whether it is progressing towards completing those goals or not. If it is not progressing, then it must be able to invoke either its own process(es) and/or external process(es) that can provide corrective action; if this is not possible, then it must be able to state that it cannot reach its goals.

2.2 Network Management Problems Caused by the Lack of Self-Awareness

Currently, network management software uses fixed data structures to interpret data; this limits the range of information that can be encoded to pre-defined concepts that can have little variation. This is exacerbated by the limitations of the syntax available in network management languages (e.g., CLI and the Structure of Management Information (SMI) [10]); in particular, there is no ability to employ richer models (such as object-oriented ones) or even to make semantics explicit. For example, it is impossible to convey critical information, such as what physical resources a given software command requires (e.g., CPU speed and amount of memory) in either CLI or SMI. Furthermore, augmenting CLI and SMI information through external means has additional problems: using a search engine relies on knowing what to look for and how to compose an appropriate query; publishing public metadata requires that users know the appropriate feed or syndication mechanism used as well as the appropriate encoding mechanism (e.g., Dublin core, RSS, or iTunes schema); publishing private metadata requires that the user understand the tagging used and its syntax.

There are other limitations as well; for example, in context-aware applications, the same data can have different meanings and/or require different actions to be taken. Current network management solutions based on SMI and CLI cannot be used in this case, as there is no ability to assign multiple definitions to a given term. More importantly, SMI and CLI lack formal semantics, which are in general required to resolve ambiguities that can arise from different uses.

2.3 Related Work

There are a number of efforts that try and address this problem. The IETF has chartered the NETMOD working group [11] to define a standard content layer for encoding network management operations in the NETCONF [12] protocol. Such a content layer requires a modeling language and accompanying rules that can be used to model the management information that is to be configured. This approach has at least two problems: (1) the approach is only valid for the NETCONF protocol, and (2) the data modeling language of NETMOD, YANG [13], has very little capability for expressing semantics associated with a configuration command (e.g., this command requires this type of hardware support, or this command will conflict with resources from the following services) and it has no ability to express higher-level features, such as business concepts (e.g., a service level agreement).

The promise of ontologies is the sharing of an understanding of a domain that can be communicated between people and application systems [14]. This has been applied in [15][16], which have used ontologies to augment network management languages with formal descriptions based on ontologies. These efforts address an important problem in network management: the proliferation of management models, each with their own language, structures, and different degrees of semantic expressiveness. The use of ontologies provides numerous benefits over current syntactic solutions, such as inference and more precise classification and querying capabilities. However, there is a problem - ontologies are defined from a particular *perspective*, which will have inherent biases and necessarily subjective features. Thus, a *mapping* is needed to translate between how knowledge is represented in the schemata that are being mapped [17][18]. Such mappings can be quite complex.

An information model is a structured representation of data independent of platform, language and protocol; a data model is tightly bound to platform, language, and/or protocol [19]. A data model is built from an information model, and is used to define how data is structured and accessed for implementation purposes. The three main models used in network management today are the Autonomic Communications Forum DEN-ng [20], the TeleManagement Forum Shared Information and Data Model (SID) [21], and the Distributed Management Task Force Common Information Model (CIM) [22]. The SID is partially derived from DEN-ng v3.5; the latest version of DEN-ng is v6.6.5.9. The CIM is not related to either DEN-ng or the SID. The TMF has had a five-year liaison relationship with the DMTF, trying to align the CIM and SID models. This work has been unsuccessful because of two important problems. First, the CIM uses its own proprietary metamodel, not that of UML. This means that the concepts used to build CIM models (e.g., classes, attributes, and relationships) are defined differently from the corresponding UML model concepts, whereas both DEN-ng and the SID use UML. In addition, the CIM is in reality a data model, as it contains technology-specific concepts, such as keys and weak relationships, which are not technology neutral. Second, patterns play a critical role in model-driven design, enabling the reuse of successful designs and helping to make models simpler and easier to learn. CIM does not use patterns; SID uses 4; DEN-ng uses many. In addition, CIM does not use roles, which both DEN-ng and the SID do. Roles make a design inherently scalable by abstracting individual users, devices, and services into roles that can be played by various managed entities. In DEN-ng and some of the SID, roles are not limited to just people; rather, they may represent resources, services, products, locations, and other managed entities of interest.

Note that there is a significant difference between the design of the DEN-ng and SID models. The top portion of the inheritance tree of the DEN-ng model was completely redesigned in version 5.5 and enhanced again in 6.0, while the root of the SID model has stayed relatively the same (since DEN-ng version 3.5). The redesign of DEN-ng was prompted to (1) enable simpler interworking with ontologies, (2) to correct some semantic ambiguities, and (3) to introduce the MetaData and Value hierarchies (both are unique to DEN-ng, and are explained in [23]).

2.4   Requirements for Self Awareness

There are a number of requirements for self-awareness. The first is an inherent desire for a self-aware entity to take actions to meet its desires. The Belief-Desire-Intention (BDI) [24][25] model is one of several models that can be used to determine the behavior of agents as they try to attain their goals. Enhancements to this model include the Belief-Obligation-Intention-Desire (BOID) [26] model, which uses feedback loops to trigger possible modifications to the original architecture. This is important to enable multiple entities to cooperate and balance their actions against their goals.

Context-awareness is required to make use of the BDI, BOID, or any other model that seeks to actively orchestrate the actions of an entity in response to changing needs and/or environmental conditions. We define context-awareness as the ability of an entity to change the functions it performs and the services it provides as a result of the receipt of external information, and have defined a robust context-aware policy model to orchestrate actions in earlier work [27][28]. This enables us to prevent the emergence of counter-productive behaviors while pursuing constructive behaviors.

However, networks are complex collections of heterogeneous hardware and software entities. Self-awareness at the network level is difficult, because (1) different entities are interconnected at different times, and (2) an entity can depend on different entities at different times. Furthermore, a problem may manifest itself at a given location that masks the root cause of the problem (e.g., that point is behind a firewall or network address translator). Hence, self-aware *communities* of entities that seek to work together to cooperatively provide services must be able to provide enough information so that a dependency analysis can be conducted to determine the root cause of the problem and instruct the appropriate set of entities to fix their part of the problem. This implies another important requirement of self-awareness: the ability of an entity to understand its own capabilities as well as the capabilities of other entities. One of the more advanced embodiments of this notion is the *self-model* defined in the CASCADAS project [29]. The self-model describes all possible behaviors of the entity; similar to FOCALE, this is done by representing desired behavior as an extended finite state machine model that incorporates actions for each state transition, and orchestrating the transitions between states (which in turn defines the behavior at any given time). The main differences between the self-model of CASCADAS and the FOCALE models are (1) CASCADAS uses a single model, whereas FOCALE uses a combination of a model and an ontology to represent the state machine and meanings of each state, and (2) CASCADAS publishes its model to other nodes, whereas FOCALE relies on a single logical model that different nodes use. The first difference enables FOCALE to attach formal definitions to augment the UML state model to enable the system to reason about the optimal path to take; this is important, for example, for choosing between equally weighted paths. The latter difference enables FOCALE to be more easily distributed in a secure manner. First, if a malicious node somehow obtained even a part of the self-model used by CASCADAS nodes, it could impart a lot of damage; this is why FOCALE does not publish its model. Second, FOCALE has more complex control than CASCADAS, in that it uses multiple nested context-aware control loops. It is impossible to publish a "piece" of a model that is context-aware without the associated context.

The increasing complexity of systems and how a given entity or set of entities should respond to changing user needs, business goals, and environmental conditions mandates the ability of a component to be aware of such changes and adapt its functionality accordingly. Traditional systems have pre-defined functionality and responses to such changes. Self-aware systems have the ability to understand their own capabilities, which enables an entity to query other entities in order to interoperate in ways that are not explicitly provided by the software of the entity, or that have not otherwise been anticipated. This implies another critical requirement for self-awareness: the ability to communicate knowledge that is not bound to a pre-defined, static knowledge base.

3   Representing Self-Awareness in FOCALE

The fundamental idea of self-aware communications in FOCALE is that each communication node "understands" the content of the information to be transferred as well as the capabilities of itself and each node that it is communicating with. This means that a given set of entities can establish a communications protocol that is optimized with respect to three metrics: (1) the needs of the current transmission (e.g., does this communication require exchanging objects, or is it a simple textual message), (2) the capabilities of the communicating entities (e.g., alternative means of exchanging data may need to be used if one or more of the communicating entities cannot support certain features and/or understand the content of the message), and (3) the current state of the system as a whole.

3.1   The FOCALE Lexicon

In order to implement this flexible and adaptable communication mechanism, we use a novel type of semantic knowledge processing that combines information/data models with ontologies to create a flexible lexicon [30]. For the purposes of FOCALE, a lexicon is defined as follows:

> *A lexicon is a collection of all words, phrases and symbols used in a language. Each word, phrase, or symbol can, in general, have a set of meanings; hence, the best or most appropriate meaning of each word, phrase or symbol can be chosen given the correct context. The lexicon contains information about the morphological variations, grammatical usage, part of speech, etymology, and social meaning of each word, phrase, or symbol.*

The above definition is based on [31], and emphasizes the holistic notion that a lexicon is not "just" a collection of words forming a vocabulary, but is rather a set of meanings as well as an associated set of relationships that, in and of themselves, provide additional meaning and understanding. Existing definitions did not provide this emphasis, although they implied it. For example, [31] says: "…that the study of word meaning reveals that the lexicon of a language is not simply an unorganized list of words. Semantic relations such as synonymy, antonymy, and the relations involved in semantic fields all serve to link certain words with other words, indicating that the overall lexicon of a language has a complex internal structure consisting of subgroups, or 'networks', of words sharing significant properties."

The FOCALE Lexicon consists of a set of objects; each object contains the fields shown in Figure 1. Each object has a name, id, a set of zero or more semantic relationships, a set of zero or more custom relationships, metadata, a set of zero or more "see" and "see also" references, a set of relationships to the model information, and a set of zero or more relationships to ontological data. Metadata define the source of the data, whether it is new or not, its timestamp, and other data that enables the FOCALE system to determine the context of the object. FOCALE uses the DEN-ng information model [20] and the DENON-ng ontology [32]; however, the method being described in this paper is generic, so other models and/or ontologies could be used instead.

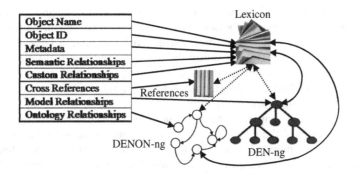

Fig. 1. Structure of the FOCALE Lexicon

Our current implementation uses three sets of standard relationships: *is-a* (defined by hyponyms and hypernyms in the DENON-ng ontology, and the generic subclass-superclass relationship in DEN-ng), *has-a* (defined by holonyms and meronyms in DENON-ng, and by aggregations and compositions in DEN-ng, and synonyms and antonyms in DENON-ng (these could be represented by associations in the DEN-ng model; however, we do not do this, as a UML association provides nothing to enforce the semantics associated with these concepts). These standard relationships form a foundation of standard semantics that all applications using FOCALE can expect to have available. Finally, we add references to external knowledge that each object can also refer to.

FOCALE uses "intelligent objects", which are objects that have a rich set of relationships that describe different aspects of what the object represents. DEN-ng consists of a set of class hierarchies that are interrelated using a common set of core classes and relationships. DEN-ng represents intelligent objects as content that are contained in a special object that functions as a container with associated metadata. Policy rules set metadata attributes, which in turn dictate the type of content that a given container can contain. This is explained in [27].

3.2 Semantic Relatedness

How do we know if two different entities are related to each other? Semantic relatedness [33] is a measure that defines how close the meanings of two entities are. It uses synonymy (e.g., "bank" and "lending institution"), antonymy (e.g., "accept" and "reject"), and other lexical relationships such as meronymy (e.g., court is a part of government). The DENON-ng ontology has been constructed to complement the DEN-ng model by building a set of linguistic relationships to link its concepts.

Traditional semantic relationships, such as those in [34] and [35], are computationally expensive, and in general are only suitable for non-real time processing. Therefore, FOCALE also uses a simpler real-time computation suitable for applications that require real-time answers by first constructing a *summary* of the salient semantic characteristics of the objects in question. Then, instead of computing *separate* semantic relatedness measures for each aspect of an object and combining these (using an appropriate weighting factor) to derive the overall semantic relatedness between two objects, each object is instead summarized; this enables a *single* semantic relatedness computation to be performed (of the summary of each object). This has a significant performance benefit, as managed objects in a network can have a large number of attributes and relationships. By correlating the real-time and non-real-time semantic relatedness values of an entity by using (for example) a hybrid reinforcement learning algorithm, we can then fine tune the summarization process to take into account inaccuracies discovered by the learning algorithm.

In order to perform a comparison between the semantic summaries of two objects, we build a set of each of the object's class, property, and association names, extend each by mapping to a common lexicon, and then perform a set of semantic relatedness tests between the two sets. We currently use WordNet [36] as an approximation to this, because of its strong Application Programming Interfaces that enable us to integrate its features into our autonomic manager. WordNet is a semantic lexicon for the English language that combines the features of a dictionary and a thesaurus to support automatic text analysis. It groups related nouns, verbs, and other parts of speech into sets of synonyms (called synsets) that each represent one underlying lexical concept. Different relationships link the synsets to each other. This is in sharp contrast to standard references that list different parts of speech alphabetically.

3.3 Modifications to Computing Semantic Relatedness Using WordNet

WordNet contains a number of different measures for semantic relatedness and semantic similarity. For a specialized domain such as network management, tests have revealed three important characteristics that help determine which of these should be useful.

The first characteristic is that the *depth of the hierarchy is usually irrelevant*, since DEN-ng employs strict classification mechanisms to organize its contents, and hence generates deep taxonomies. The second characteristic is that the *use of the is-a relation by itself is not strong enough*, due to the presence of vendor- and device-specific terminology. This often results in words that are not contained in the lexicon, and so the only way to realize that they are equivalent to existing concepts is to use semantic relationships that identify terms that can be semantically related to each other. The third, and most important, characteristic is that *many levels of the DEN-ng hierarchy are much denser than others* (e.g., the group of nodes describing roles that people can play is much denser than the group of nodes describing roles that locations can play, even though the same concept (role) is the root of both of these hierarchies). Hence, it is intuitively apparent that siblings that are located in a dense neighborhood of concepts will be more closely related to one another than those that are located in more sparsely populated neighborhoods *independent of their relative depth in the hierarchy*. Note that this goes against several different previous semantic similarity measures, such as [34] and [35], which incorporated distance and depth into their measurement. The result of these three characteristics is that a new measure of semantic relatedness, specifically for use in analyzing information and data models that exhibit irregular information content that is independent of the depth of their structure, must be developed. This will be completed in a future paper.

4 Implementing Self-Awareness in FOCALE

Recall our definition of self-awareness: the ability of an entity to understand its own behavior as well as that desired of it. Most existing autonomic systems use a control loop to collect information regarding the state of the entity being managed. The problem with this approach is that sensing and interaction is directed *towards the controlled element itself* and *not towards the environment of the system.* This will be examined by comparing FOCALE to both the IBM and the CASCADAS models.

4.1 The IBM Approach

In IBM's autonomic computing architecture [7], a model of the environment does not exist; hence, the IBM approach is limited to a pre-defined model of known functionality. In contrast, FOCALE has two models – one of a FOCALE node and one of the environment in which a node is operating. This enables more precise policies and constraints to be developed for each; in particular, it facilitates representing changed functionality when the context of a node changes.

However, there is a more fundamental problem: most control loops have limited intra-loop interaction mechanisms. For example, in [7], the control loop is limited to performing *sequential* operations; this is shown in Figure 2. In this approach, there is no opportunity for data being monitored to be properly oriented towards changing goals. As we observe mismatches between what was desired and what actually happened, we have to change our orientation to provide new corrective actions.

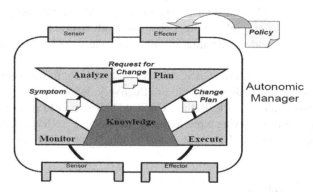

Fig. 2. The IBM Control Loop

4.2 The CASCADAS Approach

Figure 3 shows the control loop from the FP7 CASCADAS program. Autonomic Elements (AEs) have a "common" part that communicates using a set of standard interfaces that is also exposed to the outside world, and a "specific" part that uses dedicated interfaces to provide component-specific functionality (hence, only other AEs that need those functions will implement these dedicated interfaces). Specific interfaces contain semantic descriptions of the set of features that a given AE can

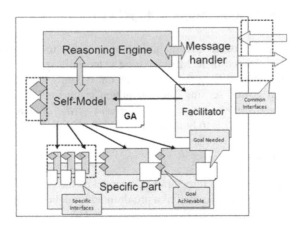

Fig. 3. The AE of CASCADAS

perform, and the conditions and actions required to accomplish each feature. The use of semantic features is not provided in the IBM approach. This enables the CASCA-DAS AE to use semantic routing (i.e., a recipient is addressed using its semantic properties) instead of using its logical or physical address. Each AE also has a "self-model", which defines the possible states and their associated transitions; this self-model is *published* to other components using a specific protocol that can describe the semantics of each state. The self-model can be *dynamically adapted* using the Facilitator, in response to (for example) context changes. Such changes are analyzed using the Reasoning Engine, and the Facilitator will adjust the model using one or more actions.

IBM uses a closed control loop. CASCADAS concluded that this is incorrect, since if there is no a priori knowledge available to effectively define control purposes and tasks, closed control cannot work. Rather, CASCADAS strives to support *emergent* functionality (instead of following a pre-defined "architecture"). Hence, CASCADAS uses a *local* control loop for self-awareness, and a global control loop for environment awareness.

4.3 The FOCALE Approach

The IBM architecture only has a model of the operation of a node, and does not provide a model of the environment. This prevents the IBM approach from being aware of environmental changes and adapting to them. In contrast, FOCALE has two models – one of a FOCALE node and one of the environment in which a node is operating. This enables separate policies and constraints to be developed for each; in particular, it facilitates represent changed functionality when the context of a node changes. This is similar to CASCADAS, except for one important feature: models are *not* published in FOCALE, as previously mentioned.

Like CASCADAS, FOCALE implements *dynamically adaptable* control loops, as shown in Figure 4. However, FOCALE inserts two important functions between the monitoring and analysis functions. The first normalizes heterogeneous data into a common form so that data from multiple types of sensors can be integrated to form a more complete description of the current environment. This function is critical for network management, because network devices are inherently heterogeneous, and use different programming models and languages. The second function *orients* these data into the current context. The orientation involves using inference functions to determine if these data can be related to other parts of this system or other components present in the environment. This enables FOCALE to detect any changes to the context of the entity being governed as well as to the system, and then *adjust its governance mechanism* accordingly. This takes the form of context changes selecting new policy rules to be enforced, as explained in [23][28].

The normalization and orientation functions deserve further attention. One of the more difficult problems in network management is to harmonize and integrate management data from different vendor devices that use different data structures and data organization to convey the same or similar concepts. FOCALE handles this problem as shown in Figure 4. Management data is processed by a set of parsers, implemented using agents, and turned into a set of XML data. This is then translated into a XML form suitable for interpretation by the autonomic manager. The Translation Logic first constructs a graph, whose nodes consist of model elements and ontology concepts that are joined by edges that represent how related they are from a semantic point of view. The set of models and ontologies are related to each other using the lexicon described in Section 3.1. The translation logic applies a suitable set of transformations to convert the raw XML output of the parser into a structured markup language for use in autonomic applications [27].

FOCALE's control loops are also different compared to CASCADAS. An outer, or macro-control loop, is used to ensure that only policy rules applicable for the context at hand are used; an inner, or micro-control loop, is a variant of the Observe-Orient-Decide-Act (OODA) control loop [37], and is used to govern the functionality of the managed entity. Adaptation uses context-aware policy rules to determine both the specific components of the control loop as well as how each component functions. For example, a threshold comparison could be changed to a semantic relatedness test depending on the type of data, state, and context. This is shown in Figure 5.

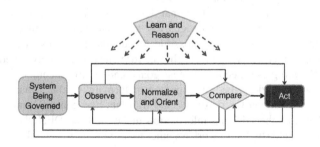

Fig. 4. The FOCALE Adaptive Control Loops

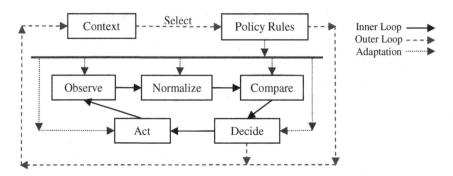

Fig. 5. The Inner and Outer FOCALE Control Loops

Since the action may be directed at a different managed entity (which, for example, could have been the root cause of the observed problem), the control loops could be changed (e.g., the original loop could be suspended or terminated and a new loop created). This can be done programmatically as well as through the use of different types of learning and reasoning algorithms. This is unique to FOCALE.

Business goals and objectives can be directly related to the system using context-aware policy models [23][28] that use the Policy Continuum [27][38] to relate the needs of different constituencies (e.g., business, network, and programming people) that use *different terms* to each other. This is another unique aspect of FOCALE. For example, it enables business people to describe services using business concepts, such as revenue; this can then be translated to a form that network engineers can use and implement (e.g., traffic classification and conditioning configuration commands). This adaptation is reinforced by the self-governing nature of FOCALE, in that the system senses changes in itself and its environment, and determines the effect of the changes on the currently active set of business policies.

5   Conclusions and Future Work

This position paper has explored the concept of self-awareness and its applicability to network management. We argue that self-awareness, which is the ability of an entity to understand its own behavior as well as that desired of it, is critical for making progress in current network management scenarios, and mandatory for those of the Future Internet. This is because it is impossible to adequately represent semantics in current network management languages; this in turn means that networked systems cannot adapt to changing user needs, business goals, and environmental conditions.

In this paper, we have described an approach to formalizing the semantics of self-awareness by using a lexicon to coordinate and translate between different knowledge sources. FOCALE uses the DEN-ng information model and the DENON-ng ontology because they have been designed to work together to provide consensual knowledge in a formal form. We use the well-known concept of *semantic relatedness* in conjunction with a novel methodology to build a graph-theoretic representation of knowledge. This gives us a flexible and extensible implementation that can incorporate changes to our knowledge base as we learn from experience from observing our deployed system.

Future work will concentrate on further evolving our self-awareness model and enhancing FOCALE accordingly. With a robust self-awareness model, we will then revisit how goals are specified, and make appropriate architectural changes. This will lead to a new model of self-governance, where both the system being governed as well as the governing system can be modeled and dynamically adjusted as necessary.

Acknowledgments. This work is sponsored in part by the WCU (World Class University) program through the Korea Science and Engineering Foundation funded by the Ministry of Education, Science and Technology (Project No. R31-2008-000-10100-0). This work is also partially sponsored by Science Foundation Ireland under grant number 08/SRC/I1403 (FAME).

References

1. Clark, D., et al.: NewArch: Future Generation Internet Architecture, NewArch Final Technical Report (December 2003), http://www.isi.edu/newarch/
2. Blumenthal, M., Clark, D.: Rethinking the design of the Internet: the end to end arguments vs. the brave new world. ACM Transactions on Internet Technology 1(1), 70–109 (2001)
3. Feldmann, A.: Internet clean-slate design: what and why? ACM SIGCOMM Computer Communication Review 37(3) (July 2007)
4. Harrington, D., Preshun, R., Wijnen, B.: An Architecture for Describing Simple Network Management Protocol Management Frameworks, RFC3411, STD0062 (December 2002)
5. Cisco, http://www.cisco.com/warp/cpropub/45/tutorial.htm
6. Tauber, A.: The Biological Notion of Self and Non-self, The Stanford Encyclopedia of Philosophy, http://plato.stanford.edu/entries/biology-self/ (accessed May 16, 2009)
7. IBM, An Architectural Blueprint for Autonomic Computing, vol. 4 (June 2006)
8. Strassner, J.: Autonomic Networking – Theory and Practice. In: 20th Network Operations and Management Symposium (NOMS) 2008 Tutorial, Salvador Bahia, Brazil (2008)
9. Strassner, J., Agoulmine, N., Lehtihet, E.: FOCALE – A Novel Autonomic Networking Architecture. ITSSA Journal 3(1), 64–79 (2007)
10. SMI defines the grammar for writing an SNMP MIB. It is defined by RFCs 2576, 2578, 2579, and 2580, all of which can be downloaded using the following form, http://www.mibdepot.com/downloads/rfcs/rfc25xy.txt (accessed on May 17, 2009)
11. IETF, http://www.ietf.org/html.charters/netmod-charter.html (accessed May 14, 2009)
12. IETF, http://www.ietf.org/html.charters/netconf-charter.html (accessed May 14, 2009)
13. IETF, http://www.ietf.org/internet-drafts/draft-ietf-netmod-yang-05.txt (accessed May 14, 2009)
14. Fensel, D.: Ontologies: Silver Bullet for Knowledge Management and Electronic Commerce. Springer, Heidelberg (2003)
15. Wong, A., Ray, P., Parameswaran, N., Strassner, J.: Ontology Mapping for the Interoperability Problem in Network Management. IEEE Journal on Selected Area in Communications 23(10), 2058–2068 (2005)
16. de Vergara, J.E.L., Villagrá, V.A., Ascensio, J.I., Berrocal, J.: Ontologies: Giving Semantics to Network Management Models. IEEE Network 17(3), 15–21 (2003)

17. O'Sullivan, D., Wade, V., Lewis, D.: Understanding as We Roam. IEEE Internet Comput-
    ing 11(2), 26–33 (2007)
18. Shvaiko, P., Euzenat, J.: A Survey of Schema-based Matching Approaches, Technical Re-
    port DIT-04-087, Informatica e Telecomunicazioni, University of Trento (2004)
19. Pras, A., Schoenwaelder, J.: On the Difference between Information and Data Models,
    RFC 3444
20. Strassner, J.: DEN-ng Model Overview. In: Joint ACF, EMANICS, and AutoI Workshop
    on Autonomic Management in the Future Internet, May 14 (2008)
21. TM Forum, http://www.tmforum.org/browse.aspx?catID=1684
22. DMTF, CIM Schema,
    http://www.dmtf.org/standards/cim/cim_schema_v2201/
23. Strassner, J., de Souza, J., van der Meer, S., Davy, S., Barrett, K., Raymer, D., Samudrala,
    S.: The Design of a New Policy Model to Support Ontology-Driven Reasoning for Auto-
    nomic Networking. Journal of Network and Systems Management 17(1) (2009)
24. Rao, A., Georgeff, M.: Modeling Rational Agents within a BDI Architecture. In: Proceed-
    ings of the Second International Conference on Principles of Knowledge Representation
    and Reasoning (1991)
25. Bratman, M.: Intention, Plans, and Practical Reason. CSSL (March 1999)
26. Broersen, J., Dastani, M., Hulstijn, J., Huang, Z., van der Torre, L.: The BOID Architec-
    ture: Conflicts between Beliefs, Obligations, Intentions and Desires. In: Proceedings of the
    Fifth International Conference on Autonomous Agents, pp. 9–16 (2001)
27. Strassner, J.: Enabling Autonomic Network Management Decisions Using a Novel Semantic
    Representation and Reasoning Approach, Ph.D. Thesis, Waterford Institute of Technology
    (2009)
28. Strassner, J., de Souza, J.N., Raymer, D., Samudrala, S., Davy, S., Barrett, K.: The Design
    of a Novel Context-Aware Policy Model to Support Machine-Based Learning and Reason-
    ing. Journal of Cluster Computing 12(1), 17–43 (2009)
29. Manzalini, A. (ed.): Report on state-of-art, requirements, and ACE model, Deliverable 1.1,
    CASCADAS program (September 2007)
30. Atchison, J.: Words in the Mind: An Introduction to the Mental Lexicon. Wiley-Blackwell,
    Chichester (2003)
31. Akmajian, A., Demers, R., Farmer, A., Harnish, R.: Linguistics – An Introduction to Lan-
    guage and Communication. MIT Press, Cambridge (2003)
32. Martin Serrano, J.: Management and Context Integration based on Ontologies for Perva-
    sive Service Operations in Autonomic Communications Systems, Ph.D. thesis, Universitat
    Polítechnica Catalunya (2008)
33. Budanitsky, A.: Lexical semantic relatedness and its application in natural language proc-
    essing. Technical Report CSRG390, University of Toronto (1999)
34. Jiang, J., Conrath, D.: Semantic Similarity based on Corpus Statistics and Lexical Taxon-
    omy. In: Proceedings of the International Conference on Research on Computational
    Linguistics, Taiwan, pp. 19–33 (1997)
35. Lee, J., Kim, M., Lee, Y.: Information Retrieval based on Conceptual Distance in IS-A
    Hierarchies. Journal of Documentation 2, 188–207 (1993)
36. Fellbaum, C.: WordNet – An Electronic Lexical Database. MIT Press, Cambridge (1998)
37. Boyd, J.R.: The Essence of Winning and Losing, June 28 (1995)
38. van der Meer, S., Davy, S., Davy, A., Carroll, R., Jennings, B., Strassner, J.: Autonomic
    Networking: Prototype Implementation of the Policy Continuum. In: 1st IEEE Interna-
    tional Workshop on Broadband Convergence Networks, pp. 1–10 (2006)

Goal-Based Service Creation Using Autonomic Entities

May Yee Chong[1], Björn Bjurling[1], Ramide Dantas[2], Carlos Kamienski[2],
and Börje Ohlman[3]

[1] Swedish Institute of Computer Science, Sweden
{bgb,may}@sics.se
[2] Universidade Federal de Pernambuco, Brazil
{ramide,cak}@gprt.ufpe.br
[3] Ericsson Research, Sweden
Borje.Ohlman@ericsson.com

Abstract. This paper presents an approach for facilitating the setting-up and management of new multi-organizational telecom services. We are addressing factors that currently impede the development of new complex telecom services. One factor is the gap between high-level business goals and low-level network management policies making it hard for business managers to quickly implement new business ideas. A second factor, due to the trends towards outsourcing and multi-organizational structures, is the increasing complexity of the services which leads to high demands on the management environments. These factors translate into high costs and long time-to-market for the introduction of new complex telecom services. As a suggestion for a solution to these issues, we propose a goal-based approach towards self-management of complex telecom services. In our suggestion lies a new breed of network devices called Autonomic Entities which should be able both to orchestrate services fulfilling given goals, and to refine and combine goals for the purpose of self-management. This paper focuses on how Autonomic Entities can be combined via a goal combining method for the creation of new services. Our approach is illustrated with examples and an application to a scenario.

1 Introduction

The telecom industry is highly dependent on the ability to quickly deploy and manage services on all levels, ranging from low-level network services to high-level business services. Currently, services on the different levels are designed and managed by different teams, possibly belonging to different organizations. This set-up leads to a number of problems concerning current network management practices. Coleman *et al.* [1] list problems such as *long time-to-market* (most new services take between 6 to 18 months to deploy); a *lack of visibility into end-to-end processes*; and an *inability of today's systems to efficiently relate the network with the service and the customer*. There are also trends both towards an increased demand for interoperability between network and content providers

J.C. Strassner and Y.M. Ghamri-Doudane (Eds.): MACE 2009, LNCS 5844, pp. 29–43, 2009.
© Springer-Verlag Berlin Heidelberg 2009

and towards a proliferation of multi-vendor networks, while at the same time it is crucial to be able to efficiently monitor and control the performance of such complex services. This accentuates the growing need for bringing business service management and network management practices closer together. Taking these factors into account, we see an increasingly complex network management environment, and it is to this background the telecom industry is increasing its focus and effort in trying to improve the manageability of their networks.

In this paper, we present a suggestion for a solution to the challenges with the increased complexity of network management. We are in particular tackling the issues that arise in connection with multi-organizational service deployment and management. When multiple organizations are required to collaborate in the provision of a service, it is crucial to be able to efficiently monitor and control the performance of the service while still permitting each organization to retain internal management of its subservices. We suggest a goal-based approach where we introduce a new breed of network devices called *Autonomic Entities* (AE). AEs should be able to refine high-level goals into lower level goals assigned as responsibilities to *subordinate* AEs to fulfil. In turn, subordinate AEs will be able to refine their goals and assign them to their subordinate AEs in an hierarchical fashion. The status of the fulfilment of subgoals is continuously communicated upwards in the hierarchy, which allows for continuous adjustments in the assignment of subgoal in an AE. We believe that this architecture will result both in self-managing AEs and a decentralized and scalable network management for the telecom industry. We further believe that our solution will lead to significant reductions both in cost and in time to market for new telecom services, as it aims at alleviating some of the obstacles in cross-organizational service deployment.

The contribution of this paper is that it gives a framework for specifying goals and it describes an architecture for the usage of goal-specifications in AE self-management and service creation via goal refinement and goal composition.

Section 2 gives the necessary preliminaries. Section 3 builds upon and formalizes the concepts in our earlier paper [2]. Sections 4 and 5 extend our previous paper [2] by giving our accounts for goal composition and goal refinement. Section 6 explains the self-management aspects of AEs. In Section 7 we apply our framework to a scenario. Section 8 gives a brief account of related work. Conclusion and future work are given in Section 9.

2   Preliminaries

2.1   Services and Service Level Agreements

We use the term service in the sense of Kotler [3] where it is any act or performance that one party offers another party. We assume in the spirit of WSDL [4] that services can be described via their inputs and outputs, i.e. for a given initial system state, a service brings about a particular desired system state.

For Service Level Agreements (SLA), we draw from IBM's language for *Web Service Level Agreements (WSLA)* [5] which is used for regulating web service provisioning and monitoring. An SLA is a contract between two parties (a *provider* and a *consumer*) whose terms include, among other items, a definition of the service and a number of SLA parameters. An SLA parameter has a name, a type and a unit, and it is associated with a metric. We pay particular attention here to the so-called Service Level Objectives (SLOs). An SLO specifies that a particular system state should be obtained at some time period. The system state is described as an expression involving one or more SLA parameters.

2.2 Policy-Based Management and Autonomic Computing

Policy-based Management (PBM) is an approach used to simplify the management of networks and systems by establishing policies for dealing with likely situations [6]. PBM separates the rules governing a system's functionality from its implementation, allowing dynamic change in behaviour without recoding. The area of policy refinement is receiving an increasing interest in the research community, and has been identified as a key area to enable PBM [7]. The aim of refinement is to enable network administrators to specify only high level (business level) policies and goals, and let the system (semi-) automatically refine these into enforceable low level policies and configurations.

The complexity of current networks has driven major players in the IT industry to look for solutions that reduce the burden of managing such large, heterogeneous systems. Companies such as IBM, HP, and Microsoft are researching technologies that should enable self-* capabilities, for example self-configuration, self-optimization, self-healing and self-protection. Such capabilities should ultimately result in systems that can manage themselves, requiring human intervention only for higher level business decisions.

IBM's Autonomic Computing initiative [8] has published concepts for autonomic systems. A key concept is the Autonomic Element, which consists of one or more Managed Resources and an Autonomic Manager that controls them. The Autonomic Manager accesses the Managed Resource, which can be any type of hardware or software resource, through a touchpoint, sometimes called a manageability endpoint, which is a consistent, standard manageability interface for accessing and controlling a Managed Resource [9].

3   Autonomic Entities

3.1   Goals

We will use the term 'goal' on several system levels, ranging from low-level network goals to high-level business goals. The definition of 'goal' by Kavakli *et al.* is general and it suits our intended usage of the term: a goal is "...*a desired condition potentially attained at the end of an action (or a process)*" [10]. We elaborate on this definition by saying that a goal is *a condition potentially attained at some desired point in time and potentially maintained for some desired duration of time.* A goal is said to be *fulfilled* by a service whenever the service can be used for bringing about the condition described by the goal.

3.2   Autonomic Entities

An Autonomic Entity (AE) is a collection of network elements (*"...facility or equipment used in the provision of a telecommunications service."* [11]) where exactly one of the network elements is designated as the *governor* and the other elements are called *subordinates* of the AE.

We propose that an AE itself is a network element. Being a network element, an AE is not restricted to a single physical device—it could consist of several devices, be a process, or be a software module. A *composite AE* is an AE where at least one its subordinates is an AE. If an AE is not composite, then it is called *atomic*. Two AEs may share any number of their subordinates, as illustrated in Figure 1. If an AE (or a network element) A is a subordinate in an AE B, then we say that A is *subordinated to* the governor of B, and that the governor of B is a *higher-level governor for* A.

An AE has the ability to perform one or several services. These services are composed of the services that its subordinates can perform. If a service that an AE is able to perform also fulfils a goal G, then we say that G is a *(goal-) capability* of the AE. The *capabilities* of an AE are all the goals it can fulfil. For fulfilling a goal, an AE may require *supporting services*. An AE requires supporting services when it is unable to perform the services by itself. For example, an ordering service may require a supporting billing service. The supporting services required by an AE are expressed as goals called *obligations*.

In a composite AE, a subordinate AE communicates its capabilities to the governor. For each of the communicated capabilities, the subordinate AE also communicates to the governor the corresponding obligations and service specific *required input*. For example, a delivery service may require as input the pick-up and delivery coordinates.

In an atomic AE (AAE), the capabilities of the subordinate network elements are assumed to be expressed in terms of policies encoding the operations executable by a device. Information from policies are translated to capabilities and announced by AAEs. In our examples, we use a router equipped with the Auto-QoS feature [12] as a subordinate of an AAE. This feature provides the means of configuring QoS for VoIP traffic on a router using specific commands such

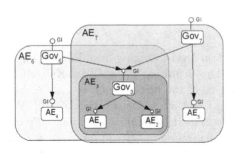
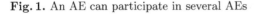
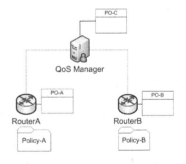

Fig. 1. An AE can participate in several AEs   **Fig. 2.** VoIP QoS Service

as 'bandwidth 512' and 'auto qos voip'. Both operations encoded in the policy are actions that need to occur for the AAE to fulfil the goals of providing a minimum amount of bandwidth (BW) for VoIP traffic.

An AE A receives requests for its services as goals either from its higher-level governor or from a set of business goals given by a user, called the *Business Service Manager*. A goal that is received by an AE is called a *goal-proposition*, a *received goal*, or a *given goal*.

The governor of an AE both receives the goals that are given to the AE and orchestrates the capabilities of its subordinates to achieve the assigned goal. These governor activities are supported by three 'governor-functionalities' we call *goal composition*, *goal refinement*, and *communication*. These three functionalities are at the core of the self-management capability of AEs, as described in Section 6. *Goal composition* is used for combining capabilities of subordinate AEs and is elaborated in Section 4. *Goal refinement* is used for orchestrating the capabilities of the AE by decomposing a given goal into subgoals such that the subordinates of the AE are capable of fulfilling the subgoals. Goal refinement is covered in Section 5.

The *communication* from a governor to its subordinates has three purposes: to specify the goals that it wants the subordinates to fulfil; to acquire information that guides the refinement process; and to tell subordinates which performance parameters that it wants to be monitored. In Subsection *3.4* below, we will use the framework of SLAs to give more formal definitions to all these concepts.

3.3   The AE Cycle

The relation between the governor of an AE and its subordinates, called the *Governance Relation*, evolves with the processes of goal composition and refinement. We describe the evolution in three phases. Upon receiving a goal, the AE enters into the *Discovery Phase* where goal composition occurs and the governor gathers the capabilities of subordinates and network elements. In the *Negotiation Phase*, the governor starts to refine the given goal into a set of subgoals. One or more subordinates may have the capabilities to achieve the same subgoal, in which case, these subordinates are *potential* candidates for the governor to form SLAs with. The governor proceeds to request for the cost from potential subordinates and selects the *preferred* subordinates based on the lowest cost received. The AE enters into the *Operational Phase* when the governor forms SLAs with the preferred subordinates. An AE transits between the three phases during self-management.

3.4   Communication and Service Level Agreements

In this subsection, we use the framework of SLAs in order to formalize the communication between the governor and the subordinates in AEs. We take as our point of departure IBM's definition of WSLA [5]. In order to avoid confusion, we introduce new names for the concepts we use in this paper even though in many cases there are similar concepts already present in WSLA.

An SLA is formed in terms of the information contained in two *announce-ments*: a *consumer service level objective (CO)* and a *provider service level ob-jective (PO)*. The CO and the PO are on a conceptual basis closely related to Service Level Objectives in WSLA, and they are made up of three types of items we call *goal-parameters, goal-constraints,* and *goals*. We assume that re-sources are identifiable by some definite set of parameters (e.g., a printer could be identified by the parameters paper, ink, and power).

A *goal-parameter* is a pair *(name,md)* where *name* uniquely identifies a re-source parameter, and a *md* is a *measure description*. A *measure description* (roughly similar to WSLA's notion of *metric*) describes a measure of a resource parameter and it is given by a triplet *(name, type, unit)*, where *name* is an iden-tifier of the measure, *type* is the set of possible values of the measure (roughly similar to WSLA's notion of *type*) and *unit* is the unit of the measure.

A *goal-constraint* is a tuple $(p, md, range, trig, time)$ where p and md form a goal-parameter (p, md); *range* is a subset of the possible values of the measure described by md; *trig* is a specification of when to measure the resource param-eter p (*trig* could be a schedule or some specific time point); and where *time* specifies a time period when the measure (given by md) of p should lie in the set of values given by *range*. A *goal* is a set of goal-constraints.

A *Provider Service Level Objective (PO)* of an AE describes the capabilities of the AE; the required inputs that it needs in order to perform the services that define its capabilities; and a set of *obligations* (describing the goals that need to be fulfilled by supporting services) for the activation of its capabilities. More formally, a PO is a triple (K, R, C) where K is a set of goals representing a set of capabilities, R is a set of goal-parameters representing the required input, and C is a set of goals such that $K \cap C = \emptyset$ representing the obligations that need to be met for fulfilling the goals representing the set of capabilities.

A *Consumer Service Level Objective (CO)* describes a goal that the governor of an AE wants to have fulfilled by one of its subordinate AEs; a specification of the inputs the governor the AE needs for its goal-refinement process (called *cost-parameters*); and a specification of the parameters that the AE needs to have monitored during the fulfilment of the goal (called *feedback*). More formally, a CO of an AE is a triple (G, P, F) where G is a goal, P is a set of goal-parameters representing the cost-parameters, and F is a set of goal-parameters where each $(name, measure) \in F$ signifies a requirement that the resource parameter iden-tified by name should be measured according to the measure *measure* and that monitoring data should be communicated to the governor.

3.5   Satisfaction and Goal-Matching

Satisfaction and goal-matching support the goal-composition and goal-refinement processes, and they are defined in terms of *compatibility* of goal-constraints. Two goal-constraints $c_1 = (p_1, m_1, range_1, trig_1, \tau_1)$ and $c_2 = (p_2, m_2, range_2, trig_2, \tau_2)$ are said to be *compatible* if $p_1 = p_2$ and $m_1 = m_2$ (i.e., goal-constraints contain-ing the same goal-parameter). If c_1 and c_2 are compatible, $\tau_1 \subseteq \tau_2$, and $range_1 \subseteq range_2$, then c_1 is said to *satisfied by* c_2. Let g_1 and g_2 be two goals. If for all goal-constraints c in g_1 there is a goal-constraint in g_2 that satisfies c, then g_1 is said to be *satisfied by* g_2.

If c_1 and c_2 (as given above) are two compatible goal-constraints, then we say that $c_1 + c_2$ is the *composed constraint* $(p_1, m_1, range_3, trig_3, \tau_3)$ where $range_3$ is the interval obtained from the addition of $range_1$ and $range_2$. The addition operator is dependent on the type of resource. In this paper we will not have space to go into the details about $trig_3$ and τ_3 other than saying that they represent a suitable trigger for monitoring of, and a suitable time-period for, the new goal-constraint. (We can ignore triggers and time-periods by the simplifying assumptions that all triggers are identical and that all time periods are identical.)

Let g_1 and g_2 be two goals and assume that g_1 contains n goal-constraints. Then the process of *goal-matching* of g_1 and g_2 creates a new goal g_3 obtained from g_1 by the process of first traversing the goal-constraints $c_1, \ldots, c_n$ in g_1 and successively either keeping c_i or replacing c_i with $c_i + c$ whenever there is a goal-constraint c in g_2 such that c_i and c are compatible, and after the traversing, including in g_3 all the constraints in g_2 that are not compatible with any constraint in g_1.

4   Goal Composition

Let A be an AE. Goal composition (for A) is the process of finding the joint capabilities of the subordinates in A. The joint capabilities are presented as the PO of A. A second effect of goal-composition is that an obligation O published by one subordinate A_1 may be satisfied by a capability of another subordinate A_2. By this, the joint PO will not have to include the obligation O. Goal composition is thus performed in terms of goal-matching and satisfaction.

Assume that A_0 is an AE with subordinates A_1 and A_2 and let PO_1 and PO_2 be the POs of A_1 respectively A_2. Goal-composition is used for combining PO_1 and PO_2 into the PO PO_0 of A_0, that is, to join the capabilities of A_1 and A_2 and present the joint capability as the capability of A_0. We describe here the construction of PO_0 from the information contained in PO_1 and PO_2.

The governor uses goal-matching in the composition of the capabilities in PO_1 and PO_2, as described in Section 3.5. The governor runs through the capabilities C in PO_1, trying to find a capability in PO_2 that can be matched with C. The new goals resulting from goal-matching are included in PO_0, as are all the capabilities that could not be matched. The required input of PO_0 is the union of the required inputs in PO_1 and PO_2. The set of obligations in PO_0 is the union of the obligations in PO_1 and PO_2.

As an example of goal composition by goal-matching, consider the goal capabilities of two subordinate entities where each entity offers a minimum BW of 512kbps at a constant bit rate in a VoIP traffic scenario. The joint capability is the offer of a minimum BW in the range of 0 to 1024kbps. On the other hand, if two subordinate entities have different capabilities, such as QoS for VoIP traffic and P2P traffic, then the goal-parameters are different and the capabilities cannot be combined.

Table 1. Composed Goals from Obligation-satsifying Goal Capabilities

PO of A_1	PO of A_2
$<c_1>,<i_1>,<o_1>$	$<c_3>,<i_3>,<o_3>$
$<c_2>,<i_2>,<o_2>$	

PO of AE
$<c_1,c_3>,<i_1,i_3>,<o_3>$
$<c_2>,<i_2>,<o_2>$
$<c_3>,<i_3>,<o_3>$

Goal composition also occurs when the obligations of one subordinate are satisfied by the capabilities of another subordinate. Consider again a governor with two subordinate entities, A_1 and A_2, if A_2 has goal capabilities that satisfy the obligations of A_1, the governor composes the capabilities of A_2 and the obligations of A_1 and so hides the obligations of A_1 in the joint PO. Obligations that cannot be satisfied by other subordinate entities are included in the joint PO. Table 1 shows the POs of two entities A_1 and A_2. A_1 announces two goal capabilities, c_1 and c_2, with their respective inputs (i_1 and i_2) and obligations (o_1 and o_2). Similarly, A_2 announces its goal capability, c_3, with its required input, i_3, and obligation, o_3. Assuming that the goal capability c_3 of A_2 satisfies the obligation o_1 of A_1, the PO for the joint capability of the AE, advertised by the governor, is the result of composing the two POs of A_1 and A_2 where the obligation o_1 is satisfied by c_3 and therefore not included in the AE PO.

4.1   VoIP Example—Goal Composition

In this subsection, we use a VoIP scenario to illustrate the process of goal composition at the atomic level. We will also use this example for goal refinement in Section 5 and self-management in Section 6. The system consists of a QoS manager with two router devices (RouterA and RouterB in Figure 2) placed in parallel for load balancing purposes and guarantees a minimum amount of BW for VoIP traffic. The goal-capabilities of each router is the provision of a minimum BW within the range of 0-512kbps for VoIP traffic. This goal-capability is announced by each router (in their respective POs - PO-A and PO-B) as a goal-constraint $c_A = c_B = (VoIP, BW, [0, 512], t, \tau)$ where VoIP identifies a resource parameter, BW is a measurement of bandwidth with the unit kbps and where measures are added arithmetically, [0,512] is the constraint on the measure, t is a trigger function, and τ is the time-period during when the constraint should hold. The required input in this case is given by a goal-parameter (VoIP, BW). The goal-parameter signifies that the router needs to know the requested BW-measure for the VoIP service.

The QoS manager formulates its own capability by composing the capabilities of the subordinate routers. Since the goal-constraints in the capabilities of both routers are compatible, we use goal-matching to compose their capabilities. The two ranges in c_A and c_B are added, resulting in the new range [0,1024]. The composed goal consists of the single goal-constraint $(VoIP, BW, [0, 1024], t, \tau)$, which is the capability published by the QoS manager in its own PO.

5   Goal Refinement

Goal refinement is performed by the Governor of an AE, to derive subgoals achievable by its subordinate entities, in order to fulfil the goal assigned to it. The Business Service Manager specifies the goals he wants the system to fulfil in a CO, which contains a set of goal constraints. The Governor receives the set of goal constraints from the BSM, performs refinement and in turn offers COs to its subordinates. In this section, we will explain the process of goal refinement by the system and the formation of SLAs between governors and its subordinates.

A governor receives POs from its subordinates during the Discovery Phase. POs are composed and no agreements has been formed at this stage. When the governor is given a CO containing a set of goal constraints from higher level governors, its role is to search for potential subordinates that can satisfy the given goals. In this Negotiation Phase, a CO with goal constraints and cost inquiries is formulated by the governor and sent to potential subordinates.

The governor uses the cost received from potential subordinates as input to a reasoning process. The outcome of the process is the optimal refinement of goals for the governor and the selection of preferred subordinates from among the potential candidates to form an SLA. The formation of an SLA between the governor and preferred subordinates will be able to fulfil the given objective at a minimal cost. This cost is propagated upwards for higher level governors to perform their own reasoning process. In the case where the governor is the user of the system (the BSM), cost information is not propagated upwards. The governor proceeds with SLA formation with preferred subordinates and the AE enters into the Operational Phase.

5.1   VoIP Example—Goal Refinement

The user of the system specifies his goal which is to obtain a minimum BW of 512kbps for VoIP traffic. The QoS manager on receipt of this goal that needs to be fulfilled, refines it using the knowledge of the capabilities previously advertised by subordinates (RouterA and RouterB) in their PO. The QoS Manager poses its goal requirements to the routers using a CO. An SLA is formulated when the goals of the QoS Manager can be fulfilled by the goal capabilities of the routers.

The QoS Manager can arrive at a number of possible refinement alternatives. We consider three of these possibilities. It can choose to form an agreement with either RouterA or RouterB to provide a minimum BW of 512kbps for VoIP traffic. Another refinement possibility is to form an agreement with both routers for a minimum BW of 256kbps each. The costs incurred from the formation of an agreement with the subordinate AEs may differ in each alternative, and is taken into consideration by the governor during the refinement process.

6   Self Management

The essence of autonomic entities is their ability to self manage. This not only requires AEs to self-configure in order to maintain its ability to fulfil given goals, it also requires self-optimization to better utilize resources available. In this section, we consider the situations that require a governor to perform self-management.

Self-configuration is invoked when the terms in an SLA no longer hold due to a consumer's *increased goal requirements* or a provider's *decreased goal capability*. A goal requirement is increased when the ranges in constraints on goal-parameters are extended, i.e. a wider range of values or a larger value. A provider's capability is decreased when the constraints on the goal-parameters are restricted, i.e. a smaller range of values or a smaller value.

In self-optimization, the terms in the SLA between a consumer and provider remains adequate and does not necessitate the modification, creation, or termination of SLAs for continued goal fulfilment. However, this binds capabilities of providers which will not be used to satisfy goal propositions of consumers. By relinquishing unused resources, they can be used by other consumers in the introduction of new services or improving existing services. As a consequence, self-optimization reuses existing AEs, maximizes the potential of their capabilities and contributes to the lowering of costs in the introduction of new services. Conflicts may occur during refinement and self-management processes and governors need to ensure that the resources are not overallocated.

6.1   Self-configuration

When a consumer increases his goal requirements, the governor of the AE determines the additional resources required to fulfil the new goal. This is accomplished by comparing the previous goals assigned to it and agreed upon in the SLA with the new goal assigned from the higher level governor (HL-Gov). The governor performs refinement using previously obtained cost information as well as POs of subordinates to determine the minimal additional costs that will be incurred to fulfil the additional resources required. SLAs are then modified, newly formed, or terminated depending on the optimal refinement pattern. Returning to our VoIP example, given that the QoS Manager has initially formed an SLA with RouterA for 512kbps of minimum BW, an increase in the goal proposition to 768kbps from BSM will require the QoS Manager to find subordinates to accommodate for the additional 256kbps of BW for VoIP traffic.

An SLA stipulates the goals that the AE, as a provider, has to fulfil for the HL-Gov and the monitoring of goal constraints. When goal constraints can no longer be satisfied due to reduced AE capabilities, feedback has to be provided. In addition, HL-Govs receives a new PO with updated goal capabilities.

The governor compares the previously agreed goals in the SLA with the goal capabilities in the new PO. It needs to determine the best self-configuration procedure so as to continue fulfillment of the terms of agreement in its SLA with its HL-Gov. Goal composition also reoccurs with modified capabilities from the new PO and this information is propagated upwards to higher level governors.

The governor as a consumer has to find other subordinates (providers) to be able to compensate for the reduced goal capabilities. It accomplishes this by performing refinement. This could result in the formation of a new SLA, with or without the termination or modification of the current SLA.

6.2   Self-optimization

In self-optimization, when a consumer reduces his requirements, the existing SLA formed between the providers and consumer remains valid as the providers are still able to fulfil the goals of the consumer. Based on the previous costs information obtained from the providers, the governor performs refinement to find the optimal refinement pattern to minimize costs. This may free up resources for AEs, which can be used for other services. In the VoIP example, the QoS Manager receives the new CO from BSM when he decides to reduce its requirements to a minimum BW of 256kbps for VoIP traffic. As a result of the new CO, the QoS Manager performs refinement based on the costs information it inquired previously and determines the best optimum refinement pattern for the new goal. We consider two refinement possibilities. First, a reduction of BW from 512kbps to 256kbps in SLA with RouterA. Second, termination of the SLA with RouterA and formation of a new SLA for 256kbps with RouterB.

When a subordinate increases his capabilities, it announces its new PO. A governor on receipt of a new PO from a subordinate, recomposes its own PO and propagates this to its own HL-Gov. The governor uses previous costs knowledge to perform refinement and determine the optimal refinement pattern.

7   Application to the Virtual Flower Scenario

We illustrate our refinement process using the Virtual Flower Scenario developed in previous work [2]. The scenario shows how existent services across different organizations can be aggregated to form a new end-user service. The new service, called "Virtual Flower" or VF, lets a customer send virtual or real flower bouquets to his/her mother on Mother's Day. The subservices for VF include a customer order interface, a flower-delivery service and a messaging service. A virtual bouquet consists of an MMS message showing a picture of a flower bouquet chosen by the customer. For the real flower service, the customer requests for a type of flower bouquet to be delivered to a specific location. A third party service provided by a flower-delivery vendor must be contracted for the delivery of the real flower bouquet.

A Business Service Manager (BSM) interacts with the autonomic entity through its *Governance Interface* (GI) [2]. Internally, this autonomic entity is composed of a governor *VFGov* and other autonomic entities (See Fig. 3). VFGov is responsible for utilizing the capabilities of subordinates in service creation. *Order* is the AE responsible for handling customer orders for virtual and real flower bouquets; Messaging *MSG* provides the MMS service; Florist *FD* delivers real bouquets to the customer's mother.

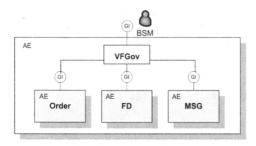

Fig. 3. Autonomic Entities in the Virtual Flower scenario

7.1   Composition Application

In the discovery phase, each subordinate AE (Order, FD and MSG) provides a
set of goal capabilities with required inputs and obligations. These are encapsulated in their respective POs and communicated to VFGov. VFGov composes
its own PO from the subordinate POs and in turn, announces it to the BSM.
Within this composition, we look particularly at how capabilities of MSG satisfies the obligations in FD. The obligation specified in the PO advertised by
FD indicates that it needs a supporting messaging capability to deliver a text
message within a certain time limit after the successful bouquet delivery. The
VFGov finds matching parameter and measure descriptions within the goal capabilities advertised by MSG. Hence VFGov advertises to the BSM the goals of
providing order handling (by Order), flower bouquet delivery (by composing FD
and MSG) and text messaging (by MSG).

7.2   Refinement Application

The BSM creates a service using the advertised capabilities of the VFGov. It
specifies the goals and their required inputs for the VF Service to the VFGov,
who performs refinement using the knowledge of the capabilities advertised by
subordinates and keeping costs to a minimum. In this application scenario, since
there is only one subordinate providing the capability to satisfy the proposition,
there are no costs to be compared between potential providers.

The BSM is not required to specify all goals that are necessary to deploy the
service. The refinement process determines related goals by leveraging on obligations that have been specified. The BSM communicates to the VFGov requesting
a service with the capability of handling flower orders at a measurement rate of
100 orders/hr. VFGov matches this goal of order handling with the capability
of Order which requires an input of an ordered item, this being flowers. The
obligation in the PO advertised by Order specifies that it is able to fulfil this
capability given that there exists another entity supporting the provision of the
ordered item. Only upon the specification of the actual input item during the
refinement process, the matching of this obligation to the capability of FD can
occur. Hence, VFGov forms an SLA with Order to handle the orders of flower

bouquets, an SLA with FD for the provision and delivery of flowers and a final SLA with MSG for the delivery of acknowledgement text messages.

7.3 Self-management Application

We assume that as Mothers' Day approaches, the BSM expects an increase in demand for the VF service and responds by submitting a new CO to the VFGov for an increased order handling capability with a measurement rate of 150 orders/hr. The VFGov compares the newly assigned goal with its previous goal, and uses the subordinates' advertised POs to determine if the subordinates have sufficient capability to satisfy an additional 50 orders/hr. If so, existent SLAs are modified to accommodate the increased demand of the capabilities to fulfil the new goal assigned by BSM. If the subordinates have fully utilized their capabilities, the VFGov feedbacks to BSM of its inability to fulfil the goal.

8 Related Work

The goal-based approach presented by Bandara et. al. [13] uses goal elaboration based on the KAOS method [14] combined with abductive reasoning to infer the mechanisms by which the given system can achieve a particular goal. This provides for partial automation compared to the manual KAOS approach which can be inconsistent and incomplete [14]. A similar approach is presented by Rubio et. al. [7], using model checking to obtain the sequence of actions needed for accomplishing a goal. Lehtihet et. al. [15] presented a goal-based approach towards self-managing IP networks, by proposing a management architecture as well as extending an existing common data model that allows the network administrator to define Autonomic Elements and their respective goal specifications. These current refinement methods allow a high-level goal to be transformed into lower-level subgoals and operations which eases service creation and supports self-management. Goal concepts and formalisms such as WSMO and WSML [16] proposed by the semantic web service community share similar ideas to our proposed expressions of consumer goals and provider services. Still, more expressivity is needed to support monitoring and formation of agreements between consumers and providers.

9 Conclusions and Future Work

In this paper, we have proposed processes to facilitate service creation between organizations and to simplify the management of complex systems. By defining goals, the SLA formation process and governing functionalities, we build upon an autonomic system architecture and cater for the discovery of capabilities of autonomic entities, the matching of consumer's need to provider's capabilities and the monitoring of performances for self-management. Goals fulfilled by subordinate AEs are aggregated and coordinated to satisfy the high-level goal defined by a service manager.

With the autonomic system architecture and communication structures in place, we shall proceed with the internal workings of the governor component of the composite AE. The governor needs to be equipped with the ability to reason for the optimal refinement of a high-level goal into subgoals that will utilize the capabilities of subordinate autonomic entities at the lowest cost. This reasoning process has to take into consideration varied types of costs such as time, monetary, and other preferences. Governors will also need to ensure the correctness of the state of an AE by using techniques such as model checking.

Acknowledgements. The present work was funded by the GOPS and PB-MAN3 projects. GOPS is sponsored by Vinnova.

References

1. Coleman Parkes Research: Transforming Operations Support Systems: Trends, Issues and Priorities of Communications Services Providers (2007)
2. Berglund, A., Bjurling, B., Dantes, R., Engberg, S., Giambiagi, P., Ohlman, B.: Toward Goal-Based Autonomic Networking. In: 3rd International Workshop on Distributed Autonomous Network Management Systems (2008)
3. Kotler, P.: Marketing Management, Analysis, Planning, Implementation, and Control, 6th edn. Prentice Hall, Englewood Cliffs (1988)
4. W3C: Web Services Description Language (WSDL) 1.1 (2001), http://www.w3.org/TR/wsdl
5. IBM Research: Web Service Level Agreements (2003), http://www.research.ibm.com/wsla/
6. Verma, D.: Simplifying Network Administration using Policy-Based Management. IEEE Network 16(2), 20–26 (2002)
7. Rubio-Loyola, J., Serrat, J., Charalambides, M., Flegkas, P., Pavlou, G.: A Functional Solution for Goal-Oriented Policy Refinement. In: Seventh IEEE International Workshop on Policies for Distributed Systems and Networks (POLICY 2006), pp. 133–144. IEEE, Los Alamitos (2006)
8. Kephart, J.O., Chess, D.M.: The vision of autonomic computing. IEEE Computer 36(1), 41–50 (2003)
9. Enterprise Management Associates: Practical Autonomic Computing: Roadmap to Self Managing Technology (January 2006), http://www-03.ibm.com/autonomic/pdfs/AC_PracticalRoadmapWhitepaper_051906.pdf
10. Kavakli, E., Loucopoulos, P.: Goal Modelling in Requirements Engineering: Analysis and Critique of Current Methods. In: Information Modelling Methods and Methodologies, pp. 102–124 (2005)
11. Commission, F.C.: Telecommunications Act of 1996, Pub. LA. No. 104-104, 110 Stat. 56 (1996)
12. Cisco Systems: Autoqos - voip (2008), http://www.cisco.com/en/US/docs/ios/12_2t/12_2t15/feature/guide/ftautoq1.pdf
13. Bandara, A.K., Lupu, E.C., Moffett, J., Russo, A.: A Goal-based Approach to Policy Refinement. In: 5th IEEE Int. Workshop on Policies for Distributed Systems and Networks (POLICY 2004), pp. 229–239 (2004)

14. Darimont, R., van Lamsweerde, A.: Formal Refinement Patterns for Goal-Driven Requirements Elaboration. In: 4th ACM SIGSOFT Symposium on Foundations of Software Engineering, vol. 21, pp. 179–190. ACM Press, New York (1996)
15. Lehtihet, E., Derbel, H., Agoulmine, N., Ghamri-Doudane, Y., van der Meer, S.: Initial Approach Toward Self-configuration and Self-Optimization in IP Networks. In: Dalmau Royo, J., Hasegawa, G. (eds.) MMNS 2005. LNCS, vol. 3754, pp. 371–382. Springer, Heidelberg (2005)
16. Roman, D., de Bruijn, J., Mocan, A., Lausen, H., Domingue, J., Bussler, C., Fensel, D.: WWW: WSMO, WSML, and WSMX in a nutshell. In: Mizoguchi, R., Shi, Z.-Z., Giunchiglia, F. (eds.) ASWC 2006. LNCS, vol. 4185, pp. 516–522. Springer, Heidelberg (2006)

Achieving High-Level Directives Using Strategy-Trees

Bradley Simmons and Hanan Lutfiyya

The University of Western Ontario
Department of Computer Science
London, Ontario, Canada
{bsimmons,hanan}@csd.uwo.ca

Abstract. A strategy-tree provides a systematic approach to the evaluation of the effectiveness of deployed policy sets and a mechanism to dynamically alter policy sets (i.e., alter strategy) at run-time in response to feedback. This paper provides an overview of the strategy-tree concept and its application to a policy-based management system for a data center. Results are presented that show that the strategy-tree can be used to balance tradeoffs between high level objectives.

1 Introduction

A data center is a collection of computing resources shared by multiple applications concurrently in return for payment by the application providers, on a per-usage basis, to the data center provider [1]. The subset of resources assigned to an application is referred to as an *application environment*. An application environment can either request that resources be added or removed. The requests are sent on a regular basis (referred to as a *periodic review*) to a management entity, the Global Perspective Manager (GPM), that is responsible for resource allocation. This approach is similar to that found in existing commercial tools such as IBM's Tivoli Intelligent Orchestrator [2].

Dynamic provisioning requires complex decision making that is guided by *policies*. Often a set of policies is designed to achieve a specific business objective. Two examples of business objectives include the following: obtain a weekly profit that is greater than t_i and limit the number of SLA violations to under t_j. Little work has been done in which the efficacy of deployed policy sets has been evaluated. The work that has been done focuses on the efficacy of a single policy set (e.g., [3]) for achieving a single business objective. However, there may be multiple business objectives [4] that may need to be considered at any one time. Current research on deriving a set of policies is usually based on achieving a single high-level goal (e.g., [5]). The reason is the complexity involved in considering several high-level goals at once when deriving policies.

This paper shows that to be able to simultaneously handle a set of business objectives (*directive*) we can use the concept of a *strategy-tree* to dynamically alternate between different policy sets where a policy set is designed for a specific business objective.

J.C. Strassner and Y.M. Ghamri-Doudane (Eds.): MACE 2009, LNCS 5844, pp. 44–57, 2009.

2 Utility Function Policies

A Service Level Agreement (SLA) [6] defines indicators that characterize behaviour e.g., availability and restrictions (*Service Level Objective*) on these indicators e.g., the availability of a resource should be at least 99.9%. The SLA specifies the price to be paid by the application provider to the data center provider if the service satisfies the SLOs or from the data center provider to the application provider if the SLOs are not satisfied.

There are many ways in which a service can be priced. We use a tiered pricing scheme similar to that found in the telecommunications industry. For each application environment, i, the first price tier defines the minimal number of resources (min_i) guaranteed by the data center provider to the application environment and the price the data center $(basePrice_i)$ should be paid for these resources. If the data center is unable to provide the number of guaranteed resources as specified then a penalty $(penalty_i)$ is paid out. The second tier specifies the price $(price_i)$ of each unit allocated that is above the minimum guaranteed. There may be a limit on the number of resources (max_i) that can be had at this price. Thus the third tier may specify the price per unit above the limit imposed by max_i or have the same price as the second tier but let the GPM determine the priority in provisioning resources beyond max_i.

In each periodic review if the number of resources available exceeds the number requested, then all requests are fully provisioned. However, when this is not the case (i.e., contention for resources) the GPM dynamically generates an optimization model as follows. A request for m resources from application environment, i, is treated as m requests denoted by $r_{i0}, r_{i1}, \ldots r_{im}$. For each request from application environment, i and each available resource an optimization variable, x_{ijk}, is created. If the jth request from application environment, i, is assigned resource k then x_{ijk} is assigned one otherwise it is assigned zero. The goal is to maximize $\Sigma\ c_{ijk}{}^{*}x_{ijk}$. A description of the policy engine, which is a component of the GPM, that supports this approach is described in [1].

The coefficient c_{ijk} is computed by a utility function that assigns a value to a request. This is similar to the concept of assigning a business value discussed in [4,7]. The utility function is a policy [8]. There are many possible utility functions. Three utility functions pertinent to this paper are briefly described. For the sake of simplicity, the price per unit in the second and third tiers are the same but the GPM uses the utility functions to determine the priority in provisioning resources beyond max_i. This priority may be based on class.

For the first utility function, U_A, higher values are assigned to those requests that allow an application environment to satisfy the minimum promised by the data center provider in the SLA then to those requests that allow a data center to overprovision beyond the maximum specified in the SLA. The priority is to minimize violations.

The second utility function, U_B is designed to maximize profit. Higher utility values are assigned to requests that allow for overprovisioning especially for Gold requests. The utility values assigned to a request that would provide an application environment, i, with more requests than max_i is higher then it is for U_A where U_A assigns utility values in order to minimize violations while U_B focuses on maximizing profit.

The third utility function, U_C is designed as an approximation of the approach used by the algorithms for managing the Triggered Policy Queue (TPQ) of a PDP [3]. A key aspect of this TPQ management approach is that requests are either met in full or left in the queue. When there is contention for resources, U_C determines whether it can fully satisfy any subset of requests (i.e., to fully satisfy a request implies to provision all m resources requested by an application environment). Only the subset of all requests that maximize profit and can be fully satisfied are assigned a utility value of 1 while all other requests are assigned a utility value of 0.

3   Evaluating Utility Function Policies

This section describes an experiment to evaluate the utility functions defined in the previous section.

3.1   Experimental Data Center Setup

Three policy sets were defined: $A = \{U_A\}$, $B = \{U_B\}$ and $C = \{U_C\}$. Two AEM clients were registered with the GPM. Each client,i, had an SLA with the data center provider (i.e., $(min_i, max_i, basePrice_i, price_i$ and $penalty_i)$) are among the parameters defined in the SLA. One client AE_1 was registered as a Bronze class client with the following parameter settings (3,10,2,3,1)). A second client AE_2 was registered as a Gold class client and its SLA contained the following SLA parameter settings (3,10,6,9,3).

3.2   Evaluation

Twenty-one trials were performed. Each trial lasted 168 periodic reviews (i.e., 1 week). Each client used a Poisson generator. AE_1 uses a generator with a mean set to 3 while AE_2 uses a generator with mean set to 4. To increase variability, after every 6 periodic reviews a random number r was chosen such that when $r > 0.5$ the next 6 requests were positive (i.e., requests for resource allocation) and when $r \leq 0.5$ the next 6 requests were negative (i.e., requests to release resources). Requests were stored in a log file so that exact duplication of a given scenario's request pattern could be repeated. Each of the 21 trials was repeated three times allowing the various policy sets to be active and thus employed by the the GPM.

Hourly Net profit (HNP) refers to the summation of (profits - costs) earned by the data center provider after one hour (i.e., for a single periodic review). Cumulative Daily Net Profit (CDNP) refers to the summation of HNP over the 24 consecutive periodic reviews representing a single 24 hour period (i.e., a day). Cumulative Weekly Net Profit (CWNP) refers to the summation of HNP over 168 consecutive periodic reviews of the trial representing the 168 hour period

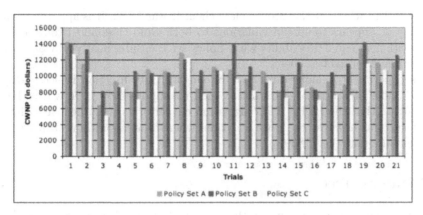

Fig. 1. CWNP for policy set A, policy set B and policy set C over 21 trials

(i.e., a week). Mean Weekly Net Profit (MWNP) is the mean of the CWNP earned over 21 trials. Mean Daily Net Profit (MDNP) is the MWNP divided by seven. Mean Hourly Net Profit (MHNP) is MWNP divided by 168.

Policy set A earned the greatest CWNP for nine of the 21 trials. Policy set B earned the greatest CWNP for 12 of the 21 trials. Figure 1 presents an overview of the results. When policy set A was employed by the GPM a MWNP of $10,298.52 was realized. When policy set B was employed by the GPM a MWNP of $11,019.76 was realized. When policy set C was employed by the GPM, a MWNP of $9,134.43 was realized. The relatively poor performance of policy set C is notable and illustrates a point. The merits of an all or nothing approach to resource allocation are questionable. Specifically, a data center provider misses out on substantial revenue generation through partial request fulfillment when it adheres to an all or nothing based approach.

Due to the poor performance of policy set C only policy sets A and B were considered for the remainder of this work. The mean of the two means (i.e., MWNP earned by policy sets A and B) was $10,659.14 and will be referred to as the target mean (TM) for the remainder of this paper.

Next, the occurrences of SLA violations were examined for both client application environments over the 21 trials under both deployed policy sets (i.e., policy set A, policy set B).

Definition 1 (SLA Violation). *An SLA violation is said to have occurred when an application environment that is currently assigned n resources such that $n < min_i$ (i.e., the minimum value of resources as specified in its SLA with the data center provider) and (i) it requests m resources such $n + m \geq min_i$ and it is allocated r resources such that $n + r < min_i$ or (ii) $n + m < min_i$ and $m > 0$ and $m \neq r$.*

The mean number of SLA violations under policy set A (over 21 trials) for the Gold class client was 10.43 while for Bronze class client it was 9.90. The mean number of SLA violations under policy set B (over 21 trials) for the Gold class client was 0.14 while for the Bronze class client it was 68.33. It is apparent that policy set A appears to spread violations to both Gold class and Bronze class clients with near equal probability while policy set B ensures nearly all violations occur to the Bronze class client.

This experiment demonstrates that no single utility function is necessarily optimal under all scenarios. This observation is supported by [3] in which they demonstrate that the HFPF TPQ algorithm outperforms the other algorithms 67% of the time; however, there are situations where other algorithms outperform it by vast amounts (i.e., 1800%).

4   Strategy-Trees

Little work has been done in which the efficacy of deployed policy sets is evaluated (e.g., [3]). Even less work has been done in which the runtime effectiveness of deployed policy sets is evaluated and policy set membership altered dynamically to improve overall performance (or to achieve higher level business objectives). To address this concern strategy-trees were introduced [9]. Strategy-trees are an abstraction that encapsulates and relates multiple strategies for achieving a directive. A policy set is the expression of how a strategy is to be implemented and is focused on a particular high-level objective. A strategy-tree assumes that multiple policy sets have been designed for achieving a directive (multiple objectives). The strategy-tree allows the policy set in use to be changed in order to better satisfy the directive.

4.1   Definition of Strategy-Tree

A strategy-tree is composed of three types of nodes: Directive, AND and OR. The following properties define a strategy-tree: A strategy-tree is defined as $ST = (V, E)$ where $V = A \cup O \cup D$ (such that A represents the set of AND type nodes, O represents the set of OR type nodes and D represents the set of directive type nodes) and $E \subset V \times V$.

Definition 2 (Strategy). *A strategy (denoted S_i) specifies one possible way of achieving the highest level directive (i.e., root node of the strategy-tree).*

A strategy, $S_i = (V', E')$, is defined such that the following properties hold:

1. The root node $r \epsilon V$ of the ST is an element of the strategy such that $r \epsilon V'$
2. A strategy consists of the nodes $V' = (A', O', D')$ such that $A' \subseteq A$, $O' \subseteq O$ and $D' \subset D$
3. The set of leaves $L \subset D'$ such that $\mid L \mid > 1$ and $\forall l \epsilon L$ the out-degree of $l = 0$
4. Every child of an AND type node $n \epsilon A$ is included in a strategy
5. One child of an OR type node $n \epsilon O$ is included in a strategy
6. The quantum attribute value q_{n-1} of a node at depth $n-1$ should be greater than the quantum attribute value q_n of a node at depth n. Further, q_{n-1} *modulo* q_n should be equal to zero.
7. Leaf nodes of the strategy-tree are bound to policy sets (a set can be empty).

8. The policy sets P_a and P_b that are bound by two leaf nodes that are both direct child nodes of the same OR node must by definition not be proper subsets of one another.

Definition 3 (Sub-strategy). *A sub-strategy (denoted S_i^2) is the component of a strategy that has at its root an OR type node. Specifically, if a OR type node acts as a choice point between n possible strategies, then there are n sub-strategies associated with those strategies emanating from the OR type node in question.*

Definition 4 (Epoch). *An epoch refers to the number of increments of the management time unit (MTU) between sequential evaluations of a given node. It is equivalent to a given node's quantum attribute value.*

An example strategy-tree (which will be described in more detail in the rest of this section) is seen in Figure 2. The strategy-tree has four alternative strategies defined: S_1, S_2, S_3 and S_4. A shorthand notation used to represent a strategy is simply to list the participant node indices for a particular strategy enclosed in round braces (this is also the notation used for sub-strategies as well). For example, $S_1 = (0, 1, 3, 5, 6)$, $S_2 = (0, 1, 4, 7, 8)$, $S_3 = (0, 1, 2, 9)$ and $S_4 = (0, 1, 2, 10)$. Strategies, S_3 and S_4 can also be thought of as one strategy $S_{34} = (0, 1, 2, *)$ with two sub-strategies: $S_1^2 = (2, 9)$ and $S_2^2 = (2, 10)$. For completeness, four other sub-strategies can be defined specifically, $S_3^2 = (1, 3, 5, 6)$, $S_4^2 = (1, 4, 7, 8)$, $S_5^2 = (1, 2, 9)$ and $S_6^2 = (1, 2, 10)$.

Every 24 periodic reviews, a decision is made based on current and past performance to determine whether for the next epoch (i.e., 24 hours) S_1, S_2 or S_{34} should be used. When strategy S_{34} is active, a second decision is made every six hours about whether sub-strategy S_1^2 or S_2^2 should be utilized for the next epoch (i.e., 6 hours). The following subsection describes these strategies in detail. Decisions require that all nodes maintain a *results* list to be able to keep track of the satisfaction of their child nodes.

4.2 Using a Strategy-Tree

In order to construct the strategy-tree in Figure 2 to achieve the weekly directive of:

– *Obtain a CWNP greater than the TM while limiting the number of SLA violations such that the ratio of violations for Gold clients to Bronze clients is within the range of 0.25 to 0.50.*

the collected data presented in section 3 is used. This data is similar to what an actual data center provider might have on hand or may have gathered through various simulation tools (i.e., [10]). This data allows for characterizations of expected client behaviour over the course of a week to be constructed.

The strategy-tree, Figure 2, presents three strategies (S_1, S_2 and S_{34}) for achieving the weekly directive. S_1 represents using policy set A while S_2 represents using policy set B. S_{34} is more complex than the other strategies and was added due to the possibility of spikes occurring (i.e., a request for greater

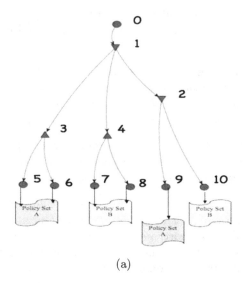

(a)

Index	Quantum Attribute Value	Member of S_n	Member of S_n^2
0	168	S_1,S_2,S_3,S_4	
1	24	S_1,S_2,S_3,S_4	S_3^2,S_4^2,S_5^2,S_6^2
2	6	S_3,S_4	S_1^2,S_2^2,S_5^2,S_6^2
3	1	S_1	S_3^2
4	1	S_2	S_4^2
5	1	S_1	S_3^2
6	1	S_1	S_3^2
7	1	S_2	S_4^2
8	1	S_2	S_4^2
9	1	S_3	S_1^2,S_5^2
10	1	S_4	S_2^2,S_6^2

(b)

Fig. 2. (a) The strategy-tree used for the experiment and (b) Table mapping node indices to their respective quantum attribute values and membership within specific strategies and sub-strategies. It is assumed that the management time unit is one hour (i.e., periodic review).

than 10 resources at a time) in Gold client requests. Specifically, S_{34} considers performance at a finer granularity of time. Every six periodic reviews, an evaluation is made with regards to whether a spike has occurred in the previous epoch and if one (or more) is detected policy set B is deployed (which ensures higher Gold client satisfaction at the cost of Bronze). However, when no spike has been detected it is the more fair, policy set A, which is deployed instead. S_{34} was added to protect against consecutive days with spikes occurring (and also to demonstrate a strategy-tree with multiple OR type nodes functioning at different temporal granularities).

SAT-elements. A SAT-element is an administrator defined mechanism for evaluating whether or not a directive, as encapsulated by a node, is being met. The SAT-element should in some way express expectations about how the system should perform under the current set of policies. The following section describes the key SAT-elements responsible for affecting the decision making process at the two OR type nodes.

The SAT elements associated with nodes 5 and 6 are evaluated each periodic review. They have been bound to policy set A. The SAT-element associated with node 5 computes the HNP (i.e., the sum of the profit for servicing AE_1 and AE_2 requests). If the HNP is below the MHNP for policy set A it signals failure to its parent node otherwise it signals success.

The SAT-element associated with node 6 is concerned with evaluating the accumulating ratio (this ratio is computed over all data for a given day so at hour 1 there is only one pair of numbers to consider but at hour 3 there are 3 pairs of numbers to consider) of Gold client to Bronze client violations. Since policy set A typically spreads violations between Gold and Bronze class clients equally, failure is signalled only if the ratio is greater than 0.50 (i.e., it exceeds the top of the range) otherwise success is signalled.

The SAT-elements associated with nodes 7 and 8 are concerned with performance in the context of policy set B being deployed (i.e., they are bound to policy set B). The SAT-element associated with node 7 computes the HNP and compares it to the MHNP for policy set B signalling failure should it be less than the value expected. Otherwise success is signalled.

The SAT-element associated with node 8 is concerned with evaluating the accumulating ratio of Gold client to Bronze client violations over a single day. Unlike policy set A, policy set B assigns SLA violations almost exclusively to Bronze class clients; therefore, should the ratio be less than 0.25 failure is signalled otherwise, success is signalled.

The SAT-element associated with nodes 9 and 10 are used to detect spikes in Gold client traffic. Should a request for greater than 10 resources be issued by the Gold client, failure is signalled, otherwise success is signalled. The SAT-element associated with node 2 evaluates its results list and should it detect any failure (i.e., a spike occurred) it signals failure, otherwise, it signals success.

DEC-elements. A DEC-element is an administrator defined mechanism, associated solely with OR type nodes, for evaluating whether to maintain or switch the current strategy and, if a change is needed, to which strategy this switch should be made. There is a DEC-element defined for nodes 1 and 2 of this particular strategy-tree.

The DEC-element associated with node 1 is the more complex of the two. This DEC-element is concerned with determining which strategy to employ each day while attempting to converge on achieving the directive of node 0. Upon execution of this DEC-element, an initial assessment of context is made. In this case, context involves (i) the current active sub-strategy (ii) an examination of the management database (MDB) to determine whether or not a spike has occurred in the preceding epoch (iii) an accumulated ratio of Gold client to

Bronze client (here, accumulated refers to an accumulation of this ratio since hour zero to present) SLA violations which is compiled based on data stored in the MDB and finally (iv) the contents of the results list. With context now established decision making begins.

If the current active sub-strategy is S_3^2 and a spike has occurred in the previous epoch then a switch is made to S_{34} with S_2^2 initially active. If the *results* list has greater than or equal to 50% success entries and the ratio is not above the target range (i.e., target range is 0.25 - .50) then the current strategy is maintained. If the *results* list has greater than or equal to 50% success entries and the ratio is above the target range then a switch to S_2 is made. If the *results* list has less than 50% success entries and the ratio is not below the target range then a switch to S_2 is made. Lastly, if the *results* list is below 50% success entries and the ratio is below the target range then the current strategy S_1 is maintained.

If the current active sub-strategy is S_4^2 and a spike has occurred in the previous epoch then a switch is made to S_{34} with S_2^2 initially active. If the *results* list has greater than or equal to 50% success entries and the ratio is not below the target range then the current strategy S_2 is maintained. If the *results* list has greater than or equal to 50% success entries and the ratio is below the target range (i.e., less than 0.25) then a switch back to S_1 is made. If the *results* list has less than 50% success entries and the ratio is not above the target range then a switch to S_1 is made. Lastly, if the *results* list has less than 50% success entries and the computed ratio is above the target range then the current strategy S_2 is maintained.

If the current active sub-strategy is S_{34} and a spike has occurred in the previous epoch but not within the past 12 periodic reviews then the sub-strategy that is activated is S_1^2 (i.e., strategy S_3). However, if there has been a violation in the previous 12 periodic reviews then sub-strategy S_2^2 is activated (i.e. strategy S_4). If no spike has occurred in the previous epoch the following considerations are used. If the ratio is below the target range then a switch to strategy S_1 is made (i.e., activate sub-strategy S_3^2). If the ratio is above the target range then a switch to strategy S_2 is made (i.e., activate sub-strategy S_4^2). If the ratio is within range then randomly switch to either S_1 or S_2.

The other DEC-element is associated with node 2 (which has a quantum attribute value of 6). Every 6 periodic reviews (i.e., one quarter of a day) an assessment of the context with regards to the presence or absence of spikes in Gold client demand is made. Six hours was selected because it evenly divides a single day into 4 quarters. A spike, while a rare event can impose a negative impact on achieving the higher-level directive. When the active sub-strategy is S_2^2 policy set B is being used (i.e., responsive). Any spike within the previous 12 periodic reviews is viewed as justification for maintaining this sub-strategy. Conversely, when the active sub-strategy is S_1^2 policy set A is being used and here any spike detected in the previous six periodic reviews is viewed as justification to switch back to the more responsive sub-strategy S_2^2.

5   Experiment

The following section describes an experiment that was performed to demonstrate the effectiveness of the strategy-tree based approach at achieving a high-level directive. Where [3] focused solely on maximizing the sum of the net financial profit earned by the service provider over a period of time, the scenario presented here considers achieving a more complex business directive. First, the data center provider wishes to earn above a target threshold value for its CWNP. Second, the data center provider wants to ensure that the ratio of Gold class to Bronze class SLA violations is kept within a defined range. The reason for this is based on the fact that both clients are important to the data center provider; however, Gold clients are to be favoured but not to the complete exclusion of Bronze clients.

To evaluate the effectiveness of the strategy-tree based approach six trials were performed each composed of three identical 168 hour runs (i.e., the request pattern generated by the first run for each client was then used by each client in each of the following two repetitions). Initially, only policy set A was deployed and the first repetition run. Then, policy set A was undeployed and policy set B deployed in its place and the second repetition run. Finally, both sets were deployed, the strategy-tree was composed in the StrategyTreeEditor, the leaf nodes were bound to their respective policy sets, SAT and DEC-element classes were generated, their logic filled in and then the final repetition was run with strategy S_1 initially set to active.

The strategy-tree based approach made the most CWNP three out of six times. It made the second most CWNP twice. It made the least CWNP once. However, it should be noted that the mean of the CWNP over six trials for the strategy-tree based approach was greater than the TM set out in the high-level directive (i.e., \$10,961.17). An overview of the six trials is presented in Figure 3.

The ratio of gold violations to bronze violations was examined next. Table 1 presents an overview of all six trials. It should be noted that the mean of the strategy-tree ratio over the six trials was 0.22. While this is not greater than 0.25 it should be noted that it is very close (and dramatically better than the single policy set alternatives).

Table 1. Ratio of Gold class violations to Bronze class violations for the strategy-tree based approach and under policy set A or policy set B separately

Trial#	Strategy-Tree	Policy set A	Policy set B
T_1	6/46	8/0	0/95
T_2	7/23	12/6	0/64
T_3	6/44	6/33	0/66
T_4	8/24	13/0	0/58
T_5	9/44	21/1	1/77
T_6	8/35	13/7	1/59

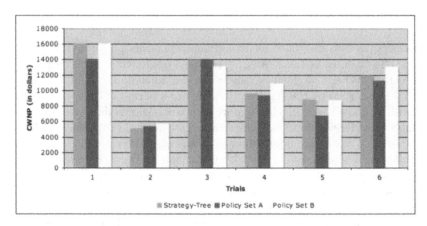

Fig. 3. CWNP for policy set A, policy set B and the strategy-tree based approach over a set of six trials

6   Related Work

The concept of policy hierarchy was first introduced in [11] and formalized in [12]. A policy-hierarchy is both a way of understanding the structural relationships between policies expressed at various levels of abstraction (i.e., consider the 6 level hierarchy of [11] or the 4 level hierarchy of [13]) and as the result of a refinement process from high-level policy to low-level policy set [12]. The concept of policy hierarchy was further developed in [14] in which it was suggested that the hierarchy should directly reflect the system architecture. A strategy-tree is similar to a policy hierarchy in that it is a hierarchical structure. However, where a policy hierarchy relates multiple policies a strategy-tree relates evaluations of achieving various directives through the deployed policy sets.

A formal, event calculus [15] based approach to policy refinement was presented in [16]. This approach used abduction to determine strategies for achieving goals at various levels of abstraction. The KAOS goal elaboration technique [17] was used to construct a goal refinement hierarchy based on system goals that was guaranteed to be logically correct. Strategies abduced from the lowest level goals represented concrete operations on specific objects in the system and could be used in the generation of low-level policy rules. A second goal-based approach to policy refinement was presented [18]. This approach also used KAOS to refine system goals; however, it differed from [16] in that it used linear-temporal model checking and verification techniques to generate policies that are automatically extracted from system trace executions. While the various approaches to policy refinements tend to result in multiple policy sets for achieving some goal a strategy-tree is concerned with evaluating these policy sets at runtime and alternating between them as required to closer achieve the high-level directive.

Goal-Oriented requirements engineering techniques have been applied by [19] to facilitate the semi-automation of high-variability business process configuration. Different business process configurations are generated based on degrees of satisfying soft goals and the relative rankings assigned to these goals by stakeholders. This work is focused at a high level of abstraction, ignores policy considerations, and is less dynamic and flexible than the strategy-tree approach.

The work proposed in [20] is similar to the strategy-tree approach in that the intent is to formally express business strategies through measurable business indicators and to dynamically alter active deployed policies in response to the dynamic evaluation of these indicators; however, the work is in its preliminary stages and the overlay environment does not yet appear to be implemented. Further, the approach is restricted to the DiffServ domain. In contrast, the strategy-tree approach is a more general and flexible framework for evaluating the effectiveness of active deployed policy sets and for altering active deployed policy set membership on the fly in response to administrator specified decision making code. Strategy-trees also attempt to evaluate what an administrator expects to be occurring (i.e., incorporate implicit assumptions underpinning policies into decision making).

7   Conclusions

This paper shows how to use strategy-tree to achieve directives where a directive is a set of multiple business objectives. A strategy-tree to achieve a weekly directive is presented in Figure 2. This strategy-tree is the basis for the experiment presented in Section 5. A preliminary prototype implementation of the strategy-tree concept was introduced in [9] and has now been integrated with the PBM framework of [21,22,1]. We will briefly discuss the work presented and future work.

Relationship between Business Objectives and Policy Sets. This paper assumes different policy sets for different business objectives. This may not always be the case. In this paper the business objectives were in conflict. Business objectives not in conflict may allow for a single policy set. This is a topic for further investigation.

Using a Single Utility Function. An alternative approach would be to use a weighted sum of the values produced by the relevant utility functions. However, the challenge is determining the weights and then determining how effective the weights are in achieving the directives. If the weights are not effective then the weights should be dynamically changed. The infrastructure to support this would be similar to what is presented in this paper.

Satisfaction Logic. The SAT-elements use a simple approach to determining if the directive is satisfied. More sophisticated approaches can be used as discussed in [4]. Future work will investigate this more closely.

Complexity of Using a Strategy-Tree. The creation of a strategy-tree requires a detailed understanding of the domain and an expectation of policy set behavior under different scenarios [9]. So far, to address complexity we have focused on facilitating the strategy-tree construction. This includes the StrategyTreeEditor module. This module is responsible for providing a GUI front end for (i) composing a strategy-tree (ii) binding leaf nodes to any available policy sets deployed in the underlying PBM framework (iii) selecting the initial *active* strategy and (iv) displaying active strategies at runtime. It also encapsulates the *evaluateCurrentStrategy* algorithm [9] (which includes the execution of SAT and DEC-elements through reflection in Java) and facilitates communication with the management database (MDB). A separate utility program is used to generate skeleton SAT and DEC-element classes from the strategy-tree representation of the StrategyTreeEditor module. It is up to the administrator to fill in the logic for these classes. Once these are filled then the strategy-tree is ready for use. We will continue to investigate the development of tools to facilitate strategy-tree construction.

Acknowledgment

Thanks to IBM Centre for Advanced Studies (CAS) in Toronto and the Natural Sciences and Engineering Research Council (NSERC) of Canada for their support.

References

1. McCloskey, A., Simmons, B., Lutfiyya, H.: Policy-Based Dynamic Provisioning in Data Centers Based on SLAs, Business Rules and Business Objectives. In: 11th IEEE/IFIP Network Operations and Management Symposium, pp. 1–4 (2008)
2. IBM Tivoli Intelligent Orchestrator,
   http://www-01.ibm.com/software/tivoli/products/intell-orch/
3. Aib, I., Boutaba, R.: On Leveraging Policy-Based Management for Maximizing Business Profit. IEEE Transactions on Network and Service Management 4, 163–176 (2007)
4. Salle, M., Bartolini, C., Trastour, D.: IT Service Management Driven by Business Objectives: An Application to Incident Management. In: 10th IEEE/IFIP Network Operations and Management Symposium, pp. 45–55 (2006)
5. Russo, A., Flegkas, A., Bandara, A., Lupu, E., Charalambides, M.: Policy Refinement for DiffServ Quality of Service Management. In: 9th IFIP/IEEE International Symposium on Integrated Network Management, pp. 469–482 (2005)
6. Moura, A., Samaio, M., Jornada, J., Sauve, J., Marques, F., Radziuk, E.: SLA Design from a Business Perspective. In: Schönwälder, J., Serrat, J. (eds.) DSOM 2005. LNCS, vol. 3775, pp. 72–83. Springer, Heidelberg (2005)
7. Beal, A., Mosse, D.: From e-Business Strategy to IT Resource Management: A Strategy-Centric Approach to Timely Scheduling Web Requests in B2C Environments. In: 3rd IEEE/IFIP International Workshop on Business-Driven IT Management, pp. 89–97 (2008)
8. Kephart, J., Walsh, W.: An Artificial Intelligence Perspective on Autonomic Computing Policies. In: 5th IEEE International Workshop on Policies for Distributed Systems and Networks, pp. 3–12. IEEE Computer Society, Washington (2004)

9. Simmons, B., Lutfiyya, H.: Strategy-Trees: A Feedback Based Approach to Policy Management. In: van der Meer, S., Burgess, M., Denazis, S. (eds.) MACE 2008. LNCS, vol. 5276, pp. 26–37. Springer, Heidelberg (2008)
10. Aib, I., Boutaba, R.: Ps: A Policy Simulator. IEEE Communications Magazine 45, 130–136 (2007)
11. Maullo, M., Calo, S.: Policy Management: an Architecture and Approach. In: IEEE First International Workshop on Systems Management, pp. 13–26 (1993)
12. Moffett, J.D., Sloman, M.S.: Policy Hierarchies for Distributed System Management. IEEE JSAC Special Issue on Network Management 11(9), 1404–1414 (1993)
13. Wies, R.: Using a Classification of Management Policies for Policy Specification and Policy Transformation. In: 4th International Symposium on Integrated Network Management, pp. 44–56. Chapman & Hall Ltd., London (1995)
14. Rubio-Loyola, J., Serrat, J., Charalambides, M., Flegkas, P., Pavlou, G.: A Methodological Approach Toward the Refinement Problem in Policy-Based Management Systems. IEEE Communications Magazine 44, 60–68 (2006)
15. Kowalski, R., Sergot, M.: A Logic-Based Calculus of Events. New Generation Computing 4(1), 67–95 (1986)
16. Bandara, A.K., Lupu, E.C., Moffett, J., Russo, A.: A Goal-Based Approach to Policy Refinement. In: 5th IEEE International Workshop on Policies for Distributed Systems and Networks, pp. 229–239. IEEE Computer Society, Washington (2004)
17. Darimont, R., van Lamsweerde, A.: Formal Refinement Patterns for Goal-Driven Requirements Elaboration. In: Foundations of Software Engineering, pp. 179–190 (1996)
18. Rubio-Loyola, J., Serrat, J., Charalambides, M., Flegkas, P., Pavlou, G.: A Functional Solution for Goal-Oriented Policy Refinement. In: 7th IEEE International Workshop on Policies for Distributed Systems and Networks, pp. 133–144. IEEE Computer Society, Washington (2006)
19. Lapouchnian, A., Yu, Y., Mylopoulos, J.: Requirements-Driven Design and Configuration Management of Business Processes. In: Alonso, G., Dadam, P., Rosemann, M. (eds.) BPM 2007. LNCS, vol. 4714, pp. 246–261. Springer, Heidelberg (2007)
20. Astorga, A., Rubio-Loyola, J.: Business-Driven Management of Policies in DiffServ Networks. In: Hausheer, D., Schönwälder, J. (eds.) AIMS 2008. LNCS, vol. 5127, pp. 180–184. Springer, Heidelberg (2008)
21. Simmons, B., Lutfiyya, H., Avram, M., Chen, P.: A Policy-Based Framework for Managing Data Centers. In: 10th IEEE/IFIP Network Operations and Management Symposium, pp. 1–4 (2006)
22. Simmons, B., McCloskey, A., Lutfiyya, H.: Dynamic Provisioning of Resources in Data Centers. In: 3rd International Conference on Autonomic and Autonomous Systems, pp. 40–46. IEEE Computer Society, Washington (2007)

A Cognitive Mechanism for Rate Adaptation in Wireless Networks

Luciano Chaves[1,*], Neumar Malheiros[1], Edmundo Madeira[1],
Islene Garcia[1], and Dzmitry Kliazovich[2]

[1] Institute of Computing – University of Campinas
Av. Albert Einstein 1271, 13083-970, Campinas, Brazil
luciano@lrc.ic.unicamp.br,
{ncm,edmundo,islene}@ic.unicamp.br
[2] DISI – University of Trento
Via Sommarive 14, I-38050, Trento, Italy
kliazovich@disi.unitn.it

Abstract. Sophisticated wireless interfaces support multiple transmission data rates and the selection of the optimal data rate has a critical impact on the overall network performance. Proper rate adaptation requires dynamically adjusting data rate based on current channel conditions. Despite several rate adaptation algorithms have been proposed in the literature, there are still challenging issues related to this problem. The main limitations of current solutions are concerned with how to estimate channel quality to appropriately adjust the rate. In this context, we propose a Cognitive Rate Adaptation mechanism for wireless networks. This mechanism includes a distributed self-configuration algorithm in which the selection of data rate is based on past experience. The proposed approach can react to changes in channel conditions and converge to the optimal data rate, while allowing a fair channel usage among network nodes. Simulation results obtained underline performance benefits with respect to existing rate adaptation algorithms.

Keywords: Wireless Networks, Rate Adaptation, Self-configuration, Self-optimization, Cognitive Algorithms.

1 Introduction

Advanced wireless technologies have emerged as the key building blocks in designing the broadband access network architectures of the future Internet. In particular, the development of sophisticated modulation schemes was a main contribution to provide high performance wireless networks. The modulation process consists in translating a data stream into a suitable form for transmission on the physical medium. Higher data rates are commonly achieved by using modulation schemes that efficiently take advantage of good channel conditions.

---

[*] The authors would like to thank FAPESP (process numbers 2006/50512-4 and 2008/07770-8) and IBM Research for supporting this work.

J.C. Strassner and Y.M. Ghamri-Doudane (Eds.): MACE 2009, LNCS 5844, pp. 58–71, 2009.

However, these schemes are more sensitive to medium quality degradation and do not perform well for long range transmissions. On the other hand, the use of robust modulation schemes leads to more resilient connections, but it results in lower data rates due to redundancy and control information overhead.

Several modulation schemes were defined in wireless technology standards to deal with unstable channel conditions. For instance, IEEE 802.11 interfaces support multiple modulation schemes, each one commonly referred for its nominal achievable data rate. Although, that standard does not specify how to dynamically select an appropriate modulation scheme (data rate) for current conditions in order to optimize network performance. This challenging issue is called rate adaptation. The absence of a standard solution motivated the proposal of several rate adaptation algorithms.

The rate adaptation process can be divided into two phases: assessing channel conditions, and then selecting the most appropriate rate based on channel quality information. Existing rate adaptation algorithms can be classified as statistics-based or signal-strength-based accordingly to their approach to measure channel conditions [1]. Statistics-based solutions infer channel quality from statistical information about frame transmissions, like frame error rate and number of retransmissions. Signal-strength-based solutions rely on wireless signal measurements as channel condition indicators. In this case, common parameters are the signal-to-noise ratio (SNR) and the received signal strength indicator.

Several rate adaptation mechanisms have been proposed and even some of them are widely used. However, current solutions still face some limitations. Signal-strength-based mechanisms suffer from the lack of a strong correlation between SNR indicator and the delivery probability at a given data rate. In addition, data rate configuration is performed at the sender node, while the signal information is available at the receiver, which leads to communication overhead [2]. These factors limit effectiveness of this approach in practice [3]. Statistics-based mechanisms are affected by the difficulty of finding proper thresholds for the selection of optimal data rate. Also, such mechanisms present long convergence time due to the use of statistical information, which leads to performance degradation on such dynamic environments [4].

In order to tackle these problems, we propose a cognitive approach for rate adaptation in wireless networks. The proposed solution, called COgnitive Rate Adaptation (CORA), is a distributed mechanism which enhances the network element with self-configuration functionality to dynamically adapt the data rate. CORA implements a cognitive algorithm to decide on the optimal rate based on a knowledge information base. It is able to quickly react to changes on channel conditions in order to avoid performance degradation, and can also ensure fair resource sharing among nodes.

The rest of this paper is organized as follows. Section 2 summarizes related work. Section 3 presents the core of the proposed rate adaptation mechanism. Section 4 aims at performance evaluation and comparison with typical rate adaptation mechanisms. Finally, Section 5 concludes the paper outlining directions for future work on the topic.

2 Related Work

One of the first solutions presented for the rate adaptation problem was the Auto Rate Fallback (ARF) algorithm, proposed by Kamerman and Monteban [5]. ARF defines fixed thresholds to increase or decrease outgoing data rate accordingly to the number of successes or failures on consecutive transmission attempts, respectively. It is a simple solution which attempts to use the highest effective data rate at each moment. However, it suffers from instability. Even when ARF reaches the optimal data rate, it keeps trying to increase the rate after a specific number of successful transmissions occurs. An improvement over ARF was proposed by Lacage *et al.* [6]. Their algorithm, called Adaptive Auto Rate Fallback (AARF), makes use of a binary exponential back off mechanism to dynamically adapt increase and decrease thresholds in order to mitigate instability resulting from unnecessary changes on data rate. Both solutions adjust the rate only to neighboring values. Also, they use the frame error rate (FER) to estimate channel quality, but they are not able to identify the cause of frame losses. As a result, they reduce the rate when a collision occurs, which is not necessary [7].

Another relevant solution is the SampleRate algorithm proposed by Bicket [3]. It periodically sends frames at data rates other than the current one to estimate the expected per-frame transmission time for each available rate. Then, it adjusts the rate to the best known one. The limitation of this approach is that it is based on a small number of probing packets, which can be misleading and trigger incorrect rate changes. It also may lead to long convergence time.

Using a complete signal-strength-based solution, the Receiver-Based Auto Rate (RBAR) algorithm [8] gets a feedback on channel quality from the receiver node to determine the optimal rate at the sender. That algorithm requires the use of the Request to Send/Clear to Send (RTS/CTS) mechanism[1] to obtain channel quality information from the destination node. This solution is not affected by collision problems and can perform well even with highly unstable channel conditions. However, the use of SNR information may lead to a problem due to the complexity of measuring it and mapping the measured value onto a specific rate [1,3]. In addition, this solution requires changes in the 802.11 protocol and introduces the RTS/CTS overhead.

The Collision-Aware Rate Adaptation (CARA) algorithm, proposed by Kim *et al.* [7], uses statistical information instead of SNR, as well it is able to differentiate frame losses. It works similarly to ARF, increasing or decreasing data rate due to consecutive successes or losses in frame transmissions, respectively. Moreover, it can use the RTS/CTS mechanism to identify the cause of frame losses. In the case that collision is the cause of frame loss, the algorithm can prevent unnecessary decrease of date rate. The rate should be decreased only if frame losses result from channel condition degradation. This approach reduces misleading channel quality information due to collisions, but introduces overhead and can lead to instability by alternating between the use or not of the RTS/CTS mechanism.

---

[1] The RTS/CTS mechanism can be used in 802.11 networks to reduce frame collisions when accessing the shared wireless medium.

The Cross-layer Rate Adaptation (CLRA), proposed by Khan *et al.* [9], considers application preferences and time constraints when deciding on the best data rate. This algorithm aims at selecting the lowest rate that can effectively meet required traffic demand of running applications. The use of equations can straightforward guide this rate selection. The problem comes when the medium allows the use of a higher rate and this algorithm selects a lower one. This behavior induces the performance anomaly problem discussed in [10]. That is, if there is at least one host with a lower rate, than the throughput of all hosts transmitting at the higher rate is degraded below the level of this lower rate.

Limitations of the aforementioned solutions are related with supporting loss differentiation to avoid unnecessary rate adjustments, avoiding complex or not realistic channel quality metrics, and preventing long convergence time. All these factors were considered in the design of the proposed cognitive rate adaptation mechanism. CORA does not consider frame loss ratio to guide rate selection. Consequently, there is no need for loss differentiation. Also, the proposed algorithm does not depend on signal strength indicators like SNR. As detailed later, CORA is built upon a cognitive algorithm that selects the optimal rate accordingly to evidenced past experience. As a result, it is able to quickly react to changes and adjust the data rate for current network conditions avoiding performance degradation.

3   Proposed Solution

In this work, we propose a cognitive mechanism for data rate adaptation in wireless networks. The proposed mechanism is built upon CogProt, a framework for cognitive configuration and optimization of communication protocols. In next subsection, we briefly describe the CogProt framework, and then we present a detailed description of the cognitive rate adaptation mechanism and its setup.

3.1   The CogProt Framework

The CogProt framework was developed considering the concept of Cognitive Networks, which has emerged as a promising paradigm to deal with performance degradation resulting from changing network conditions. Such paradigm relies on cognitive algorithms to provide dynamic reconfiguration of communication systems, through learning and reasoning, in order to optimize system-wide performance [11]. CogProt aims at implementing this concept by periodically reconfiguring protocol parameters based on recent past experience. As a result, the framework enables network nodes to dynamically adjust their configuration to avoid performance degradation. In order to do this, CogProt introduces a cross-layer cognitive plane as illustrated in Fig. 1. This plane is responsible for optimizing protocol stack parameters at different layers. Such optimization process is performed by several quality feedback loops, one for each parameter of interest.

The quality feedback loop consists in monitoring the performance of a parameter P and then enforcing reconfiguration actions to converge P to optimal

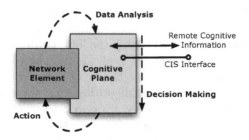

Fig. 1. Overview of the CogProt framework

operational point. This optimization process consists of three phases: data analysis, decision making, and action. During the *data analysis* phase, the cognitive plane collects performance information about the current value of the parameter P, according to a specific quality metric. Moreover, a local knowledge base is built from performance information collected at each iteration of the feedback loop in order to assist the *decision making* phase. During this second phase, the cognitive plane selects the value of P that provides the best performance, and assigns it to the mean of a random number generator that follows a normal distribution. This selection relies not only on the local cognitive information base, but also on (remote) cognitive information shared among network nodes and configuration policies for the network segment obtained from a local Cognitive Information Service (CIS). The *action phase* consists of assigning a new value to P. This value is obtained from the random number generator in the operation range of parameter $P \in [P_{min}, P_{max}]$.

This optimization process is repeated at each interval I, and continuously adjusts the mean of the normal distribution to the value of P that provides the best performance according to the performance information base. As a result, the mean of the normal distribution converges to the optimal value for P. Consequently, most of the randomly chosen values for P are optimal under current network conditions. Meanwhile, the mechanism will eventually test neighboring values (close to the mean), allowing adjustment of the parameter in face of changes on network conditions.

3.2   Cognitive Rate Adaptation

Since we have already described the CogProt framework, let us now revisit the rate adaptation problem. The proposed Cognitive Rate Adaptation mechanism (CORA) is an instance of the CogProt framework, designed to optimize the MAC layer performance by dynamically adjusting the transmission data rate. In this case, the parameter of interest is the MAC data rate (R) and the associated quality metric is the MAC throughput. CORA implements a single quality feedback loop into the MAC layer, as illustrated in Fig. 2. Each phase of this self-optimization process is explained as following.

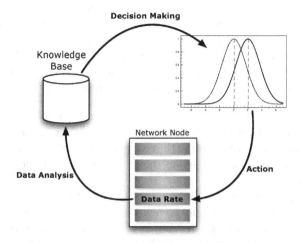

Fig. 2. Overview of the cognitive rate adaptation mechanism

Data Analysis: Performance information on each value $R_i \in [R_{min}, R_{max}]$ is maintained in the local knowledge base. Let R_c be the current value for data rate. In this phase, the mechanism measures the performance P_c obtained from using R_c in terms of MAC throughput. Then the information is averaged with an exponentially weighted moving average (EWMA) as follows:

$$P_i = (1 - w) * P_i + (w) * P_c \tag{1}$$

where P_i is the stored performance information for R_i, w is the weight assigned to immediate performance for R_c and $c = i$. That is, the measured performance for the current data rate is used to calculate the average performance for this data rate. The local knowledge base reflects the performance history for each possible value. The weight w can be used to control the relevance of recent performance information. High w values increase the effect of immediate performance information on the average performance, which enable the algorithm to quickly react in face of changes on channel conditions. Small w values lead to a more conservative behavior which results in system stability because, in this way, irrelevant transient states do not affect the convergence to the optimal operational point.

Decision Making: In this phase the mechanism decides on the optimal date rate. The algorithm looks the knowledge base up for the data rate R_i that provides the best performance. The corresponding data rate is assigned to the mean of the normal distribution. CORA algorithm does not make use of remote cognitive information or configuration policies from the CIS. The decision make process is decentralized since it relies only on information available at the network element itself, and does not require any communication with other nodes.

Action: A new random $R_i \in [R_{min}, R_{max}]$ is generated according to the normal distribution, and assigned to the MAC data rate. The standard deviation (STD) for the normal distribution defines the aggressiveness of the mechanism. The lower the STD, the more conservative is the behavior of the algorithm in trying new values for the data rate. Therefore, this parameter directly affects the convergence time and system stability.

This quality feedback loop is performed by each element at the end of a sample interval I. Several works discuss this timing consideration for channel quality measurement [1,3,6]. All of them argue that, to properly perform rate adaptation, the correlation between channels errors must be at least of the order of the sampling interval.

It is important to clarify that CORA mechanism is executed by each network element in an independent way. Besides, each element has its own local knowledge base. These features characterize a completely decentralized system, without the need of a coordinator element. Furthermore, it is feasible that elements enabled with CORA work together with elements that run/perform another rate adaptation algorithm (or none). This is possible because CORA demands neither information exchange among network nodes nor changes on the MAC protocol.

4   Performance Evaluation

In order to evaluate performance, the *Network Simulator (ns-2)*[2] was extended with CORA functionality. The performance of the proposed solution was compared against typical rate adaptation mechanisms, namely, Auto Rate Fallback (ARF) and Receiver-Based Auto Rate (RBAR). Wireless network used in experiments is configured according to IEEE 802.11g standard, using the Free Space propagation model and operating with the Destination-Sequenced Distance Vector (DSDV) routing protocol. Control frames are sent at the basic date rate (6 Mbps) and the frame size is 1500 bytes. The simulation time is 1200 seconds. The results are the average from at least 10 iterations, using a 95% confidence interval.

There are 8 available modulation schemes in IEEE 802.11g corresponding to the following nominal data rates: 6, 9, 12, 18, 24, 36, 48 and 54 Mbps. We have mapped an integer index $i \in [0, 7]$ to each available data rate $R_i \in [R_{min}, R_{max}]$. In addition, a "performance table" is implemented to store the MAC throughput information for each R_i. At start-up, the "performance table" is empty and the data rate is set to 6 Mbps as a conservative approach. At the end of each interval I, the algorithm stores performance information for the current data rate, selects the index i that corresponds to the rate R_i with the highest MAC-layer performance and then sets the mean of the normal distribution to i.

As discussed in the previous section, there are three control parameters for the cognitive mechanism: I, w, and STD. We performed simulations using different

---

[2] Available at http://www.isi.edu/nsnam/ns

combinations with these parameters, in order to select the values that provide best results. We simulated sampling intervals (I) ranging from 10 ms up to 8 s. In all scenarios, values close to 100 ms provided the best performance results. We evaluated w values ranging from 0 up to 0.9. The value 0.9 provided the best performance in terms of convergence time because it assure a higher weight to immediate past performance information. As a result, CORA is able to quickly reacts to changes on channel quality. In addition, we evaluated STD values from 0.2 up to 1.5 and the value 0.3 provided the best performance. Lower STD values allowed the algorithm to choose the optimal rate with a higher frequency (in this case, near 90%) which resulted in better performance.

4.1   Simulation Results

Scenario 1: Single Flow. In this scenario, we consider two nodes: a stationary node S and a mobile node M, as illustrated in Fig. 3. There is a single flow from S to M, with a constant bit rate (CBR) traffic source of 20 Mbps over UDP protocol. Node M starts moving away from S with constant speed of 0.25 m/s, until it reaches a distance of 300 m between them.

First of all, we evaluate the performance of each available modulation scheme. Figure 4 shows throughput as a function of the distance between nodes. Each modulation scheme is referred for its nominal rate (from Mod6 to Mod54). The presented throughput accounts for protocol overhead and frame losses. Lower data rates have greater transmission ranges. As the range increases, the signal attenuates due to fading and path loss. At different distances, there is a data rate that provides the best throughput. In this case, it is necessary to select the appropriate available data rate to maintain the highest possible throughput.

Then, we compared the throughput achieved by the three rate adaptation algorithms: CORA, ARF, and RBAR. The results are presented in Fig. 5. We can see that CORA performs better in converging to the best rate at each distance from the sender. ARF periodically tries to send frames at the next higher rate, inducing unnecessary adaptations (and consequently, losses). The RBAR performance is penalized by the use of RTS/CTS mechanism in a scenario free of collisions.

The average throughput for each algorithm and each fixed data rate is presented in Fig. 6. There is also a "maximum" value that represents the theoretical

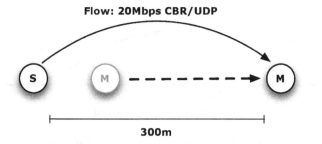

Fig. 3. Simulated topology for Scenario 1

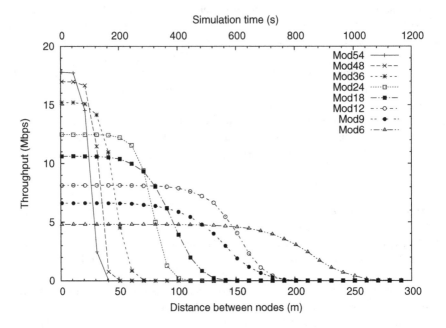

Fig. 4. Throughput over distance for 802.11g fixed data rates

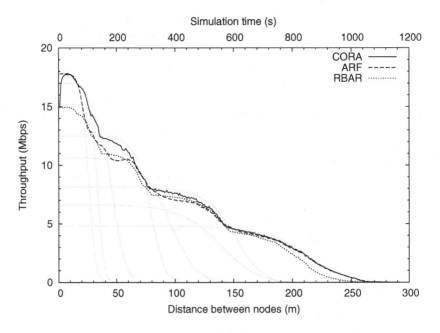

Fig. 5. Throughput over distance for each rate adaptation algorithm

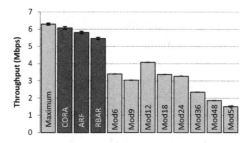

Fig. 6. Average throughput for each algorithm and fixed data rates in Scenario 1

best achievable performance when selecting always the best rate. CORA reaches up to 96% of this maximum value, outperforming ARF by 4.5% and RBAR by 11.2%.

Scenario 2: with Cross-Traffic. This scenario extends the first one by adding two nodes generating cross-traffic, which leads to collision and interference. Cross-traffic nodes are stationary, fixed at 10 meters between each other. There is a single flow between them with an intermittent CBR traffic source of 20 Mbps. Figure 7(a) illustrates this topology. Also in this scenario, CORA provides better performance than ARF and RBAR, as presented in Fig. 7(b). Collisions leaded to unnecessary rate decreases by ARF. The use of RTS/CTS mechanism in RBAR contributed to its poor performance. CORA reaches up to 96.5% of the maximum achievable value, outperforming ARF by 4.9% and RBAR by 13.1%. The fact that the cross-traffic source starts and stops repeatedly confirms the ability of CORA to quickly react to changing channel conditions.

Scenario 3: Multiple Destinations. CORA has improved support for rate adaptation involving multiple destinations. In order to evaluate that, we consider in this scenario an infra-structured wireless network with a single Access Point (AP) sending data to several stationary client nodes at different distances, as shown in Fig. 8. Throughput performance was measured considering two different topologies. The first one consists of two client nodes: one located close

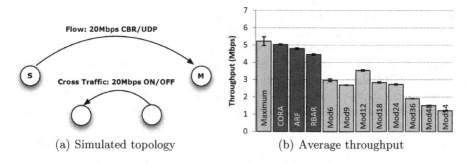

(a) Simulated topology   (b) Average throughput

Fig. 7. Simulated topology and average throughput of each algorithm in Scenario 2

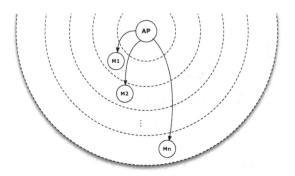

Fig. 8. Simulated topology for Scenario 3

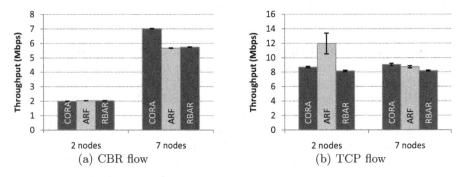

Fig. 9. Average network throughput in Scenario 3

enough to the AP such that the highest available data rate is the optimal one, while the other client is far enough such that the lowest data rate is the best one. The second topology includes seven client nodes located at increasing distances from the AP. In this case, the AP must converge to different optimal data rates when sending frames to each destination node. There are simultaneous flows from the AP to each client node using FTP (over TCP) and CBR (over UDP) traffic sources. In this scenario, CORA outperforms ARF and RBAR for up to 22%, as we can see in Fig. 9.

Figure 9(a) shows the average network throughput when using CBR flows of 1 Mbps for both topologies, with 2 and 7 client nodes, respectively. A two-client topology requires low bandwidth capacity, and all three algorithms are able to delivery frames with practically no losses. However, when the number of nodes increases, CORA shows the best performance. In the same way, Fig. 9(b) shows the average throughput considering FTP flows in both topologies. In this case, ARF provides the best performance for the 2-node topology but at the cost of unfair resource sharing as we can see in Fig. 10 and Fig. 11.

Figure 10 shows the average flow throughput in both topologies considering CBR traffic. In this scenario, node 1 is the closest to the AP. With increased number of nodes, we can see that CORA is able to provide system-wide fairness.

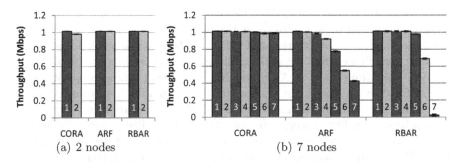

Fig. 10. Average flow throughput for CBR flows in topologies with 2 and 7 nodes

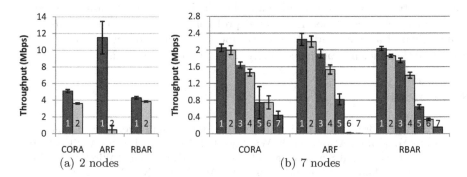

Fig. 11. Average flow throughput for FTP flows in topologies with 2 and 7 nodes

ARF and RBAR penalize nodes far away from the AP. The performance degradation for distant nodes may be gradual, as observed for ARF, or drastic, like in the case of RBAR for nodes 6 and 7.

In the case of TCP traffic, the problem of unfair resource sharing is even more critical because the high frame error rate for distant nodes caused drastic reductions on the TCP congestion window. Figure 11 presents the average flow throughput for TCP flows in both topologies. As showed before, ARF performs better for TCP traffic in the 2-node topology, but it lead to unfair bandwidth sharing as we can see in Fig. 11(a). In the case of the 7-node topology, CORA provides the best performance which is demonstrated in Fig. 11(b). CORA is the solution that provides the higher throughput for distant nodes, improving overall performance by 3.9% and 10.9% if compared with ARF and RBAR, respectively.

5   Conclusions and Future Work

In this paper, we have proposed a cognitive rate adaptation mechanism (CORA) for wireless networks. Such mechanism is decentralized and can be implemented even on devices with limited resources due to its low processing requirement. Moreover, it does not require any changes of IEEE 802.11 MAC protocol. It is also incrementally deployable, since CORA-enabled nodes can communicate with those nodes that do not implement the mechanism.

Simulation results demonstrate that CORA is able to dynamically adjust data rate always matching current network conditions. It outperforms commonly rate adaptation algorithms such as ARF and RBAR by up to 22% in specific situations. CORA gets close to the theoretical best achievable performance, and quickly reacts to changing channel conditions. The initialization is very short, and the solution quickly converges to the optimal rate. The proposed solution also is able to optimize rate adaptation even for multiple simultaneous transmissions. CORA improves fairness in bandwidth sharing, allowing communication between distant network nodes.

Future work will focus on a detailed study of how to proper setup CORA control parameters. Moreover, we will adapt the existing implementation to support multi-hop wireless networks. Additional probability distribution functions will be investigated as candidates to replace normal distribution, which may allow improving the efficiency of the cognitive optimization algorithm.

References

1. Ancillotti, E., Bruno, R., Conti, M.: Experimentation and Performance Evaluation of Rate Adaptation Algorithms in Wireless Mesh Networks. In: PE-WASUN 2008: Proc. of the 5th ACM Symposium on Performance Evaluation of Wireless Ad Hoc, Sensor, and Ubiquitous Networks, pp. 7–14. ACM Press, New York (2008)
2. Haratcherev, I., Langendoen, K., Lagendijk, R., Sips, H.: Hybrid Rate Control for IEEE 802.11. In: MobiWac 2004: Proc. of the 2nd International Workshop on Mobility Management and Wireless Access Protocols, pp. 10–18. ACM Press, New York (2004)
3. Bicket, J.: Bit-rate Selection in Wireless Networks. Master's thesis, Massachusetts Institute of Technology (MIT), Department of Electrical Engineering and Computer Science (February 2005)
4. Xia, Q., Hamdi, M.: Smart Sender: A Practical Rate Adaptation Algorithm for Multirate IEEE 802.11 WLANs. IEEE Transactions on Wireless Communications 7(5), 1764–1775 (2008)
5. Kamerman, A., Monteban, L.: WaveLAN-II: A High-Performance Wireless LAN for the Unlicensed Band. Bell Labs Technical Journal 2(3), 118–133 (1997)
6. Lacage, M., Manshaei, M., Turletti, T.: IEEE 802.11 Rate Adaptation: A Practical Approach. In: MSWiM 2004: Proc. of the 7th International Symposium on Modeling, Analysis and Simulation of Wireless and Mobile Systems, pp. 126–134. ACM Press, New York (2004)
7. Kim, J., Kim, S., Choi, S., Qiao, D.: CARA: Collision-Aware Rate Adaptation for IEEE 802.11 WLANs. In: INFOCOM 2006: Proc. of the 25th International Conference on Computer Communications, pp. 1–11. IEEE Computer Society Press, Washington (2006)
8. Holland, G., Vaidya, N., Bahl, P.: A Rate-Adaptive MAC Protocol for Multi-Hop Wireless Networks. In: MobiCom 2001: Proc. of the 7th International Conference on Mobile Computing and Networking, pp. 236–251. ACM Press, New York (2001)

9. Khan, S., Mahmud, S., Loo, K., Al-Raweshidy, H.: A cross layer rate adaptation solution for IEEE 802.11 networks. Computer Communications 31(8), 1638–1652 (2008)
10. Heusse, M., Rousseau, F., Berger-Sabbatel, G., Duda, A.: Performance Anomaly of 802.11b. In: INFOCOM 2003: Proc. of the 22th International Conference on Computer Communications, vol. 2, pp. 836–843. IEEE Computer Society Press, Washington (2003)
11. Thomas, R.W., Friend, D.H., Dasilva, L.A., Mackenzie, A.B.: Cognitive networks: adaptation and learning to achieve end-to-end performance objectives. IEEE Communications Magazine 44(12), 51–57 (2006)

OSPF for Implementing Self-adaptive Routing in Autonomic Networks: A Case Study

Gábor Rétvári[1], Felicián Németh[1], Ranganai Chaparadza[2], and Róbert Szabó[1]

[1] Department of Telecommunications and Media Informatics
Budapest University of Technology and Economics, Budapest, Hungary
{retvari,nemethf,robert.szabo}@tmit.bme.hu
[2] Fraunhofer Institute for Open Communication Systems, Berlin, Germany
ranganai.chaparadza@fokus.fraunhofer.de

Abstract. Autonomicity, realized through control-loop structures operating within network devices and the network as a whole, is an enabler
for advanced and enriched self-manageability of network devices and
networks. In this paper, we argue that the degree of self-management
and self-adaptation embedded by design into existing protocols needs
to be well understood before one can enhance or integrate such protocols into self-managing network architectures that exhibit more advanced
autonomic behaviors. We justify this claim through an illustrative case
study: we show that the well-known and extensively used intra-domain
IP routing protocol, OSPF, is itself a quite capable self-managing entity,
complete with all the basic components of an autonomic networking element like embedded control-loops, decision-making modules, distributed
knowledge repositories, etc. We describe these components in detail, con-
centrating on the numerous control-loops inherent to OSPF, and discuss
how some of the control-loops can be enriched with external decision
making logics to implement a truly self-adapting routing functionality.

Keywords: Autonomic/Self-managing Networks, self-adaptation, autonomic routing functionality, OSPF.

1 Introduction

OSPF (Open Shortest Path First, [1]) is perhaps the most successful routing
protocol for the IP suite. It is a link-state routing protocol, with two-level routing hierarchy, support for basically any type of medium IP supports, an integrated neighbor discovery and keep alive protocol, reliable link state flooding,
fast shortest path routing algorithm, support for multipath routing, etc. Accordingly, OSPF rapidly gained ground after its inception, and it has been enjoying
unparalleled popularity in the networking community to our days. Only special
environments, like extremely large ISP backbones or heterogeneous, multiproto-
col networks, are where alternatives are preferred [2].

A key enabler in the success of the OSPF routing protocol is the inherent capability for self-management built into it from the bottom up. Self-management, in

J.C. Strassner and Y.M. Ghamri-Doudane (Eds.): MACE 2009, LNCS 5844, pp. 72–85, 2009.
© Springer-Verlag Berlin Heidelberg 2009

the case of OSPF, means that the routers participating in the distributed process of IP routing perform various management tasks autonomously, independently of any higher level control function or manual intervention. A quintessential self-management operation built into OSPF is self-adaptation to the network topology at hand: OSPF routers autonomously discover network topology, disseminate topology information and compute shortest paths to produce consistent routing tables, and this self-adaptation mechanism is completely independent of external control or human supervision of any kind. There are several other self-management functionality hard-wired into OSPF, like autonomous detection of neighbors (auto-discovery), autonomous advertisement of capabilities (self-advertisement), adaptation to failures and outages (self-healing), etc. Thanks to these sophisticated self-* features, only little manual configuration is required for OSPF to perform the complex task of routing table maintenance. Once network interfaces are properly brought up and supplied with unique IP addresses, and OSPF is made aware of the interfaces it should use, the protocol is up and running, with full support for basic network routing. Only for complex operations, like link weight adjustment, multiple administrative areas, or interfacing with inter-domain routing protocols, does OSPF need special configuration and manual intervention on the part of the network operator.

One could argue, however, that in fact the autonomous capabilities built into OSPF are a bit over the point, as sometimes these self-management functions may work against, instead of cooperating with, the network operator. This is because for a network operator to achieve her network-level performance objectives, she needs to be in full control of the network. However, once OSPF with its intrinsic self-management functionality comes into the picture, the management actions taken on the part of the network operator and the self-management actions carried out by OSPF might easily end up interfering with each other. For instance, the policy of OSPF to provision the forwarding paths exclusively over shortest paths might differ from the policy seen by the operator as optimal. Thus, network operators have for a long time been working around OSPF's shortest path routing by tweaking the link weights for obtaining the desired routing pattern [3]. In other words, fulfilling network-level objectives is much easier with direct control over the configuration of the data plane and therefore, the decision logic should not be hard-wired into protocols but rather it should be re-factored into an external, pluggable control logic, which should be fed by monitoring information from the network and whose output should then be communicated back to the routers. This modularization of network fabric and control intelligence is one of the most important promises of the concept of Autonomic Networking.

For anyone to be able to incorporate OSPF into an autonomic network framework, one must need to be aware of the inherent self-management functionality built into it. Without first discovering how OSPF performs autonomous adaptation to external and internal stimuli by itself, anyone willing to deploy autonomic networking functionality on top of OSPF might easily find himself needlessly re-implementing autonomic functionality already present in OSPF, or blindly interfering with OSPF's intrinsic control-loops. The aim of this survey is, therefore, to reinterpret OSPF in an autonomic networking context. In other words, we are curious as to how well OSPF fits into the autonomic networking framework.

In what follows, we shall use the GANA framework (Generic Autonomic Network Architecture [5]), proposed by the EFIPSANS project [6] recently, as reference model for autonomic networking. GANA is an architectural Reference Model for Autonimicity and Self-Management within node and network architectures. In [5], different instantiations of the GANA approach for different types of network devices and network environments (e.g., wireless, mobile or wired/fixed) are presented, which demonstrate its use for the management of a wide range of functions and services, including both, basic network services such as autonomic Routing and autonomic Monitoring, as well as advanced services such as autonomic Mobility and Quality of Service (QoS) Management. A central concept of GANA is that of an autonomic Decision Element (DE) that implements the logic that drives a control-loop over the management interfaces of its associated Managed Entities (MEs). Thus, in GANA, self-* functionalities are always associated with certain control-loops, implemented by Decision Element(s). Additionally, GANA organizes DEs into a DE-hierarchy: the higher we go up the hierarchy of DEs, the broader the global knowledge that is required by a DE to take decisions on managing/controlling its associated MEs, which may in turn inductively trigger actions on lower level MEs down to the level of protocols.

The rest of the paper is structured as follows. First, we describe the self-* functionality embedded in OSPF and we treat the most important intrinsic control-loop of OSPF, the self-adaptation control-loop, in large detail (Section 2). We also discover the state of the art in various extensions and improvements to this intrinsic self-adaptation control-loop. The second part of the paper (Section 3) is devoted to demonstrate how OSPF could be exploited for implementing self-adaptive routing in the GANA framework, what Decision Elements and control-loops would be necessary, and we delve into some implementation details. Finally, we conclude the paper in Section 4.

2 Self-* Functionality in OSPF

Routing is the process of ensuring global reachability between IP routers and hosts. In the beginning, routing tables were provisioned manually. This practice led to daunting management complexity as networks grew, and it was quite prone to human errors. The very purpose of introducing routing protocols was to mitigate this management burden by automating the process of setting up routing tables. In some sense, autonomic networking can be seen as an extension of this idea to the extreme: make the systems themselves tackle all the management complexities, not just routing, that are otherwise difficult to handle manually. For this, the network needs to be able to self-provision and self-manage to some extent. Such self-* functionality involve, for instance, self-adaptation to changes in the operational conditions, self-healing to repair or circumvent failures, self-optimization for improving performance related aspects of networking, etc. Below, we show that many of these self-* functionalities, either only partially or in their entirety, can readily be identified in one of the most commonly known and used routing protocols, the Open Shortest Path First (OSPF) routing protocol [1]. The enumeration is given in roughly the same order as the corresponding self-* function appears in the course of the real operation of the protocol.

Auto-discovery: OSPF routers discover their immediate neighborhood by using the Hello protocol. Neighboring routers periodically exchange Hello packets, so that each router is aware of all the routers connected to any one of the links or LANs attached to its interfaces. This auto-discovery mechanism is pretty extensive, covering every aspect of routing except for one very important issue. In particular, it lacks support for box-level discovery. This means that routers do not autonomously self-detect their interfaces, and manual configuration is needed to make an OSPF router aware of the interfaces it should involve in OSPF message passing (see more on this issue later).

Self-description: OSPF routers self-describe their capabilities in the Hello packets they generate. Hello packets contain information regarding the highest version of OSPF the router's implementation supports, plus a bitfield to describe OSPF extensions the router understands. This makes it possible to eliminate the chance of mis-configuration arising from letting routers using divergent OSPF versions to speak to each other, or to deploy protocol extensions seamlessly.

Self-advertisement: Routers generate so called Link State Advertisements (LSAs) to advertise their forwarding services into the network. These LSAs convey information on the individual routers making up the topology, with their identity, attached interfaces, IP addresses, etc.; the links and LANs connecting the routers with their type (broadcast, Non-Broadcast-Multiple-Access, point-to-point); administrative link cost, etc. OSPF variants, like Traffic Engineering extensions to OSPF (OSPF-TE, [7]) and OSPF extensions in support of Generalized Multi-Protocol Label Switching (OSPF-TE-GMPLS, [8]) add their respective type of link state information to LSAs, involving the link's transmission capacity, free capacity, protection type, the forwarding services offered by the router, the multiplexing/demultiplexing capability of interfaces, etc. It is by passing these LSAs around between routers using a reliable, acknowledged flooding protocol that OSPF synchronizes routing information across the domain. This mechanism basically maintains a distributed, versioned, massively parallel Link State Database (LSDB), shared and synchronized amongst OSPF routers, which ensures that (in steady state) each router holds exactly the same copy of the network topology and thusly consistent forwarding paths are selected.

Self-configuration and self-organization: Self-configuration involves setting up and maintaining some configuration parameter by the protocol itself, that otherwise would be handled by the network operator. Self-organization is a method by which entities autonomously organize themselves into groups or hierarchies. A good example of self-configuration and self-organization in OSPF is the election of Designated Routers. In order to reduce the amount of protocol traffic on

LANs that connect multiple routers, each OSPF router synchronizes with only a single neighbor, the Designated Router (DR), instead of having to exchange signaling information with all the other neighbors. The DR is responsible for generating an LSA on behalf of the LAN. The actual DR (and the Backup DR, which is just what its name says) is elected autonomously, by means of the Hello protocol, without the need to be configured manually by the network operator.

Self-healing: An operational network is constantly subjected to disturbances from the environment, most important amongst these is the intermittent and unavoidable failures of network devices and transmission media. To come over failures, OSPF implements a simple but efficient self-healing mechanism: once a router detects that a certain node or link went down (through not getting Hello packets for a certain amount of time from a specific direction), it advertises the changed topology information into the domain, leading to a global recalculation of routing tables with the failed node or link removed from the topology. Although this self-healing mechanism might be somewhat slow due to the need to deliver the LSA to the furthest part of the network to achieve correct global response, it is highly effective in maintaining reachability as long as the network remains connected, irrespective of the number and type of failures occurring.

Self-adaptation: The most important self-management functionality implemented by OPSF is undoubtedly self-adaptation to the topology at hand. This means that routes are not provisioned statically, but instead OSPF is able to dynamically maintain correct, consistent and loop-free forwarding tables over an arbitrary topology. Self-adaptation is, therefore, the most important property of OSPF and the very purpose the protocol was designed in the first place. In the next section, we shall discuss the self-adaptation control-loop in more detail.

One could as well keep on listing the various self-* functionality built into OSPF further (e.g., self-protection, etc.), but we believe that the above examples were sufficient enough to demonstrate the richness of OSPF in terms of autonomicity. In fact, OSPF implements, either in its entirety or only partially, pretty much every possible self-* functionality, with the notable exception of box-level auto-discovery and self-optimization. The lack of self-optimization means, for instance, that OSPF is not able to readjust forwarding paths (or at least, the link costs) in order to mitigate or eliminate congestions or load-balance traffic, that is, to optimize the performance of the network. In order to equip OSPF with self-optimization functionality, we shall need to incorporate it into an external control-loop, as shall be discussed later on.

2.1   Self-adaptation in OSPF

Self-adaptation to the underlying topology, to topology changes and to other stimuli effecting network routing, is the main purpose of a routing protocol. Below, we interpret the main self-adaptation control-loop implemented by OSPF in the context and terminology of the GANA framework for autonomic networks [5].

The basic operation of the self-adaptation control-loop of OSPF is as follows. When OSPF takes off or when the underlying topology changes (that is, when a link or node goes down or comes up again), the auto-discovery mechanism of OSPF (i.e., the Hello protocol), through observing the neighborhood of the router, initiates the self-advertisement functionality to flood the (changed) network state information throughout the network. Routers, upon the receipt of new LSAs, calculate new routing tables based on refreshed routing information, which makes it possible to always self-adapt to the actual network topology.

In GANA, this self-adaptation mechanism is a typical example of a *protocol-intrinsic control-loop*, with the OSPF protocol acting as a virtual distributed Decision Element (DE) scattered all over domain. The following important autonomic networking components are involved in this control-loop (see Fig. 1):

- The *Managed Entity* is the collective set of all Routing Tables in the network, which are then used to populate the Forwarding Information Bases (FIBs). The Routing Table(s) is the entity on which the control-loop's effector operates.
- *Monitoring* of the links/interfaces and their forwarding state is implemented by the Hello protocol
- *Analyze/Plan* is broadly mapped to the process of routing table (re)calculation
- *Execution* corresponds to the process of updating the Routing Tables as well as the FIBs across the routers with the next-hops obtained during the last routing table calculation
- *Knowledge* is manifested in this self-adaptation control-loop by the collective set of the LSDBs of the routers. Note that, however, OSPF pays special attention to always keep the LSDBs at each router consistent, synchronized and up-to-date, therefore the Knowledge component is in fact replicated throughout the network instead of being unified at a central knowledge base.
- *Sensors/Effectors for higher level DEs:* the OSPF protocol supplies a number of interfaces for higher level DEs to interact with it, including (usually) a set of OSPF configuration files, a Command Line Interface (CLI) plus a versatile, standardized Management Information Base (MIB).

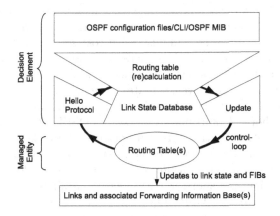

Fig. 1. Self-adaptation control loop in OSPF

2.2   Extensions to the Intrinsic Self-adaptation Control-Loop of OSPF

The self-adaptation mechanism built into OSPF is somewhat basic, although quite straight-to-the-point: it only involves tracking topology changes. However, it does not contain mechanisms, knowledge, services, algorithms or other protocol machinery to self-adapt other aspects of routing to the actual environment, or to adapt the self-adaptation control-loop itself when changing conditions make it necessary. Below, we give a brief overview of the state-of-the-art as to how the research community proposes to extend the basic self-adaptation control-loop of OSPF beyond its present capabilities. Note that the survey below lists only those proposals that build the extensions right into OSPF itself, and do not involve those ones that organize OSPF into an external control-loop with a separate Decision Element (we discuss the latter option in the next section).

Self-adaptation to changing resource availability: It has been pointed out many times as one of the major shortcomings of OSPF-type link-state routing protocols that their self-adaptation mechanism is static, as it only involves adaptation to the (changing) topology, but not to the changing operational conditions, the amount and type of actual ingress or egress traffic, availability of free resources, QoS criteria, Service Level Agreements, customer-provider and peering relationships, etc. This makes OSPF routing insensitive to the fluctuations of user traffic, or its changing/evolving embedment into a vibrant sociocultural/economic environment. The result is often suboptimal routing: traffic tends to concentrate along shortest paths while, at the same time, complete portions of the network remain under-utilized. Various attempts have been made to introduce some forms of dynamic routing into OSPF, by adding further information to the link state, most importantly, the amount of provisionable resources at network elements, and selecting routes that avoid overloaded components. A good example is the Quality of Service extensions to OSPF (QoSPF, [9]), or recent standardization efforts, like OSPF-TE and OSPF-TE-GMPLS.

Self-adaptation and multipath routing: The basic mode of operation in OSPF is to select the shortest weighted path towards a destination, where path weight is understood in terms of some administrative cost set for each network link. Where ambiguity arises (that is, when there are more than one shortest paths to a destination), one path is selected somewhat randomly. In the Equal-Cost-MultiPath (ECMP) mode, however, a router is allowed to use all the potential shortest paths to the destination, by splitting traffic roughly equally amongst the available next-hops. Unfortunately, however, OSPF-ECMP still does not qualify as a self-adaptive multipath routing protocol, because traffic is not balanced with respect to available resources along the paths. Additionally, the path-diversity of ECMP is somewhat insufficient, as in many topologies it is only a rare accident that multiple shortest paths become available to a destination. OSPF-Optimized-MultiPath (OSPF-OMP, [10]) is aimed at overcoming these difficulties: it improves path diversity by not confining itself to shortest paths but utilizing all loop-free paths instead, and it makes self-adaptation sensitive to varying operational conditions by dynamically readjusting traffic shares at individual forwarding paths with respect to actual resource availability along those paths.

Fast self-adaptation and self-healing: As mentioned earlier, the self-adaptation control-loop in OSPF involves a tedious global resynchronization of Link State Databases plus additional recalculations of the routing tables. This scheme of global, reactive response makes the convergence of the control-loop slow, which yields that the reaction to failures is a lengthy process in OSPF. Furthermore, the auto-discovery process, responsible for detecting the error in the first place, adds its own fair share of slugishness to the process (the smallest granularity of the Hello timers is 1 sec, basically increasing the convergence time to the order of seconds). To speed up convergence, a localized, proactive approach should be taken instead, and this is exactly the way the IP Fast ReRoute (IPFRR, [11]) suite of standards is set to remedy the situation. In IPFRR, OSPF pre-computes detours with respect to each potentially failing component and stores the next-hops in an alternative forwarding table. By using an explicit, fast detection mechanism like Bidirectional Forwarding Detection (BFD, [12]), discovering a failure is possible within milliseconds of its occurrence. If an error is detected, OSPF switches to this alternative table and suppresses global response by withholding the fresh LSA in the hope that the failure is transient. Should the failure go away soon after, OSPF switches back to the original forwarding table as if no failure happened. Only when a failure persists for a longer period of time, global re-convergence is initiated. IPFRR proved highly efficient in practice, bringing down to failure recovery to the order of milliseconds [13].

Self-adaptation with partial/outdated link-state information: A basic assumption lying in the heart of the design of OSPF is that the information in the Link State Database is always consistent and up-to-date. Otherwise, self-adaptation might suffer as certain destinations might become unreachable and transient or even persistent routing loops might emerge. The assumption of consistency and freshness, however, might not always hold: in fixed or slowly changing wireless networks, it would be crucial to limit the amount of signaling traffic exchanged between nodes in order to save battery power. The idea here is to tweak the self-advertisement mechanism so that routers hold precise information only in a limited vicinity, and the further they look the more inaccurate the link state information. As a packet travels hop by hop in the network, it will always see locally accurate link state, leading to, hopefully, close to optimal shortest path forwarding. For pointers on how to change the intrinsic self-adaptation of OSPF, see FishEye State Routing [14] or XL Link State [15].

3   OSPF for Implementing Truly Self-adaptive Routing

So far, we have seen that OSPF implements a solid number of self-* functions in itself, by means of control-loops embedded deep into the protocol machinery. The most important of these, the self-adaptation control-loop, is an efficient and robust control-loop and, considering the numerous extensions to this control-loop on their way to standardization and large-scale deployment, OSPF is expected to need only very little governance from higher layers to achieve its full potential. *This does not mean that OSPF on its own qualifies as an autonomic, self-managing protocol entity, only that certain functionality it embeds can be interpreted, to some extent, within the context of autonomic networking frameworks, like GANA.* Instead, to truly realize the vision of autonomic, self-managing routing, separate Decision Element(s) are needed, decoupled from OSPF and implemented in higher layers of the GANA DE-hierarchy, either because, due to implementation considerations, decision making would be very difficult to engineer into OSPF itself, or the decision making process would make use of external information that is simply not available at the lowest level of the DE hierarchy OSPF resides at in the GANA architectural Reference Model. Or, one might deliberately choose not to embed certain control-loops into OSPF in order to better modularize the architecture, to separate managed and managing functionality from each other, to easily swap/change the decision making process, etc.

Next, we discuss how Autonomic Routing is modelled in the GANA framework, and then we describe some additional control-loops to realize this vision on top of OSPF.

3.1   Implementing Autonomic Routing Following the GANA Approach

The Routing Functionality of network nodes and the network as whole can be made autonomic by making diverse Routing Schemes and Routing Protocol Parameters employed and altered based on network-objectives, changes to the network's context and the dynamic network views in terms of events, topology changes, etc. Fig. 2 depicts how the routing behavior of a node/device and the network as a whole can be made autonomic. The cloud on Fig. 2 represents an overlay or logically centralized DE(s): (1) With wider network-wide view to perform sophisticated decisions, e.g., network optimization; (2) Centralized to either avoid processing overhead in managed nodes or scalability and/or complexity problems with distributed decision logic in network elements; (3) The Elements in this cloud may be the ones that provide an interface for a humans to define network Goals and Objectives or Policies, e.g., Business Goals.

Two types of control-loops are required for managing/controlling the routing behavior. The first type is a node-local control-loop that consists of a *Function-Level Routing_Management_DE* embedded inside an autonomic node, e.g., a router. The local *Function-Level Routing_Management_DE* is meant to process only that kind of information that is required to enable the node to react autonomically and autonomously (according to some goals) by adjusting or changing the behavior of the individual routing protocols and mechanisms required to be running on the node. It reacts to "views", such as "events" or "incidents", exposed by its Managed Entities (MEs), i.e., the underlying routing protocols or mechanisms. Therefore, the *Routing_Management_DE* implements

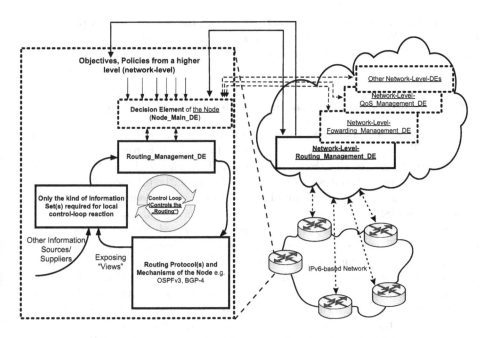

Fig. 2. Autonomicity as a feature in Routing Functionality

self-configuration and dynamic reconfiguration features specific to the routing functionality of the autonomic node.

It is important to note that due to scalability, overhead and complexity problems that arise with attempting to make the *Routing_Management_DE* of a node process huge amounts of information/data for the control-loop, logically centralized DE(s), outside the routing nodes, may be required, in order to relieve the burden. In such a case, a network-wide slower control-loop is deployed in addition to the faster node-local control-loop (with both types of loops working together in controlling/managing the routing behavior). Therefore, both types of control-loops need to work together in parallel via the interaction of their associated *Routing_Management_DEs* (one in the node and another in the realm of the logically centralized network overlay DEs). The *Node-scoped Routing_Management_DE* focuses on addressing those limited routing control/management issues for which the node needs to react fast (the faster control-loop). At the same time, it listens to control from the *Network-level Routing_Management_DE* of the outer, slower control loop, which has wider network-views and dedicated computational power, and thus is able to compute routing specific policies and new parameter values to be used by individual routing protocols of the node. The *Network-level Routing_Management_DE* disseminates the computed values/parameters to multiple node-scoped *Function-Level Routing_Management_DEs* of the network-domain that then directly influence the behaviour of the targeted MEs, that is, the routing protocols and mechanisms within a routing node. The interaction between the two types of *Routing_Management_DEs* is achieved through the *Node_Main_DE* of a node, which verifies those interactions against the overall security policies of the node. The *Node-scoped Routing_Management_DE* also relays "views", such as "events" or "incidents", to the *Network-level Routing_Management_DE* for further reasoning.

3.2 Control-Loops for Autonomic Routing on Top OSPF

Auto-discovery: As mentioned earlier, auto-discovery in OSPF lacks box-level discovery. This means that there is no way for an OSPF router to learn autonomously the set of functional interfaces it has, and configure the protocol properly on those interfaces. Unless OSPF is explicitly told so (by means of manual configuration, intervention at the CLI or through central network management), an OSPF router will not use an interface, even if, by all measures, it legitimately could. The reasons for this are multi-faceted. First, whether to run or not run OSPF on a specific interface is a crucial configuration issue, dependent on high-level network engineering policies, and it has important security implications as well. There are various configuration parameters (e.g., timers, link cost, authentication, link type, etc.) that quite commonly need manual tweaking too. Additionally, every interface must uniquely be associated with a specific OSPF area, retaining the consistency of the network via the Backbone Area, and this also must be handled through explicit configuration. Therefore, OSPF must be involved in some forms of a auto-discovery/self-configuration control-loop: an OSPF router needs to send its identity and some router-specific data upstream to the *Network-level Routing_Management_DE*, and in turn it gets back a routing profile with a complete set of configuration parameters to set, including the list of interfaces to bootstrap, timer settings, authentication keys, link costs, etc.

Self-configuration: As discussed previously, the network operator can tweak the operation of OSPF, with considerable detail and granularity, through configuration parameters. Monitoring, setting, and adjusting from time to time these configuration parameters might benefit the operation and the performance of the network. The main enabler for this is OSPF's timer mechanism, which allows the network operator to manipulate the way certain events are scheduled.

For instance, in networks with limited resources the signaling traffic generated by OSPF might put too much burden on the network infrastructure, leading to premature drainage of battery power, congestion along low-capacity links, etc. Thus, relying on monitoring data, a higher level DE might instruct OSPF to slow down LSA propagation (OSPF parameter: `MinLSInterval`, `MinLSArrival`[1] and `RxmtInterval`, see Appendix A and C in [1]). The Hello protocol could also be tweaked to generate smaller keep-alive traffic in slowly changing environments or between high-reliability interfaces where failures only rarely show up (OSPF parameter: `HelloInterval`, `RouterDeadInterval`). To save precious battery power at wireless nodes, OSPF routing table recalculations could also

---

[1] These two parameters are protocol constants, or architectural constants, which means that they are not marked as user configurable in the OSPF standard, though, they could be easily made to be so in implementations.

be throttled leading to smaller computational burden on the CPU (note that the OSPF standard does not provide an OSPF parameter to throttle SPF calculations, but implementations usually do).

Self-optimization: In OSPF, link weights completely determine, through the shortest path algorithm, the emergent forwarding paths and thus have crucial impact on the way user traffic flows through the network. Even though link costs are set to a constant value almost universally in today's OSPF deployments, it does not necessarily has to be so. Constant weight setting (either to a default constant or a static value reciprocal to the link capacity) leads to a routing that is completely and adversely independent of the operating conditions (i.e., the load at network links, the amount of incoming user traffic, etc.), which often leads to inefficient data forwarding.

In order to improve the performance of the network, link costs could (and should) be regularly updated to better reflect the actual operational circumstances, and this could be done by organizing OSPF into a self-optimization control-loop. In this control-loop, either the router itself (in particular, the router's *Node-scoped Routing_Management_DE*) or the the *Network-level Routing_Management_DE* could readjust the link costs (OSPF parameter: `Interface output cost`). The difference between the two approaches is the amount of monitoring data based on which link cost recalculation can be done. If the link costs are readjusted at the node level, only knowledge available to that node can be used in the readjustment. For instance, cost of overloaded or heavily used local interfaces could be increased, while the cost of underutilized local links could be decreased, but no information on the load at links at remote parts of the network could be used in this process. Unfortunately, careless local intervention, apart from flooding the network with excess signaling traffic, usually leads to global oscillations and instability [16]. Hence, it is better to readjust link weights at the network level [3], [17]. It is important to note that, as theoretical results confirm, it is hopeless to drive the network right to optimal performance, due to the inherent limitations and inflexibility of shortest path routing. Yet, one can go pretty close to the optimum [3], and this is more than enough in most of the cases.

Self-organization: Routers in an OSPF domain can be structured into so called areas, with complete topology information available inside the area but only limited, summarized information flooded between the areas. This makes it possible to reduce the signaling overhead of OSPF, better modularize the network, eliminate excess signaling in stub areas (parts of the network with a single ingress/egress router), etc. In a bandwidth-constrained network, the area structure could be readjusted every time it is believed that the signaling overhead of OSPF could be reduced that way. Note that, however, changing area boundaries on the fly may lead to routing-loops and transient spillage of reachability, making this self-organization function less appealing. Curiously, even the *raison d'être* of areas has been questioned quite vigorously in the near past [18].

Inter-domain self-adaptation: Interaction between intra-domain and inter-domain routing has for a long time been a hardly understood and thus heavily researched question [19]. The two are not completely independent from each other: a simple change of an intra-domain forwarding path might have far-reaching consequences, causing routing updates in a significant portion of the entire Internet. Additionally, many of the changes of external routes are advertised into the routing domain, often causing the the fluctuation of ingress traffic and/or outgoing traffic. This makes it important to try to readjust the interaction between intra- and inter-domain routing based on a detailed knowledge of topology, monitoring data, network mining data, predicted profiles, AS paths, BGP policies, etc. However, currently there exists very little understanding as to how changing some aspects of this interaction effects the rest of the network, which makes designing, implementing and optimizing such an inter-domain self-adaptation control-loop quite a task.

4   Conclusions

In this paper, we have seen that one of the most widely known network protocols, the OSPF routing protocol, includes a fair number of traits that qualify as some forms of self-management. Apart from the main control-loop, the self-adaptation control-loop, we have shown examples of auto-discovery, self-healing, self-configuration, etc. Taking a wider look, it turns out that many network protocols in existence today, especially telecommunication protocols, are designed around some forms of a control-loop. A good example is the venerable TCP flow control protocol. However, these control-loops were designed piece-meal and were deeply hidden in the very substrate of the network protocol engines. A basic promise of the emerging concept of Autonomic Networking is to give a new and enlightening way to think about network-management, thus facilitating for implementing advanced and enriched self-manageability of network devices and networks. This allows us to re-engineer *implicit* control-loops, that are currently buried deeply into many protocol engines, into *explicit* control-loops, communicating over standardized interfaces with heavily optimized and flexible decision making logics changeable and swappable on the fly.

In the case of OSPF, we undertook the first steps of this process. We identified the most important control-loops intrinsic to OSPF, which makes it possible to open up the protocol and incorporate it into external control-loops, where necessary. We found that very little external control is needed for the basic operation of OSPF. One such issue is auto-configuration with proper routing profiles for bootstrapping. In the case of self-optimization, another area where OSPF is in need for external control, we found that decision making has the chance to be more effective at higher levels of the network management hierarchy, due to the greater amount of knowledge that can be made available to the optimization algorithm. For further information on standardizing autonomic behaviors, DEs, MEs and their interactions over well-defined control loop hierarchies, see the EFIPSANS project page at [6], or consult [5].

We believe that taking a fresh look at OSPF from the standpoint of autonomic networking, identifying some of its intrinsic self-* functionality and discovering the ways these functions can be enriched, three ends we tackled in this paper, will help better understand the fundamentals of how protocol-intrinsic and external control-loops need to interact wherever necessary, and it will be instructive in engineering a truly self-adaptive future routing architecture, as the one illustrated in this paper.

Acknowledgement

The first author was supported by the Janos Bolyai Fellowship of the Hungarian Academy of Sciences. This work was carried out as part of the EU FP7 EFIP-SANS project [6]. The authors would like to thank for the anonymous reviewers for their insightful comments, which greatly contributed to advance the quality of the paper.

References

1. Moy, J.: OSPF Version 2. RFC 2328 (April 1998)
2. Oran, D.: OSI IS-IS Intra-domain Routing Protocol. RFC 1142 (February 1990)
3. Fortz, B., Thorup, M.: Internet traffic engineering by optimizing OSPF weights. In: INFOCOM (2), pp. 519–528 (2000)
4. Ballani, H., Francis, P.: CONMan: a step towards network manageability. SIGCOMM Comput. Commun. Rev. 37(4), 205–216 (2007)
5. Chaparadza, R., Papavassiliou, S., Kastrinogiannis, T., Vigoureux, M., Dotaro, E., Davy, A., Quinn, K., Wodczak, M., Toth, A.: Creating a viable evolution path towards self-managing future internet via a standardizable reference model for autonomic network engineering. In: Proceedings of FIA 2009, Prague (May 2009)
6. The EFIPSANS Project, http://www.efipsans.org
7. Katz, D., Kompella, K., Yeung, D.: Traffic Engineering (TE) Extensions to OSPF Version 2. RFC 3630 (September 2003)
8. Kompella, K., Rekhter, Y.: OSPF Extensions in Support of Generalized Multi-Protocol Label Switching (GMPLS). RFC 4203 (October 2005)
9. Apostolopoulos, G., Kama, S., Williams, D., Guerin, R., Orda, A., Przygienda, T.: QoS Routing Mechanisms and OSPF Extensions. RFC 2676 (August 1999)
10. Villamizar, C.: OSPF Optimized Multipath (OSPF-OMP). Internet Draft (February 1999)
11. Shand, M., Bryant, S.: IP Fast Reroute Framework. Internet Draft (February 2009)
12. Katz, D., Ward, D.: Bidirectional forwarding detection. Internet Draft (February 2009)
13. Enyedi, G., Szilágyi, P., Rétvári, G., Császár, A.: IP Fast ReRoute: Lightweight Not-Via without additional addresses. To appear at INFOCOM 2009 (May 2009)
14. Pei, G., Gerla, M., Chen, T.W.: Fisheye state routing: A routing scheme for ad hoc wireless networks. In: Proceedings of ICC 2000, New Orleans, LA (June 2000)
15. Levchenko, K., Voelker, G.M., Paturi, R., Savage, S.: XL: an efficient network routing algorithm. SIGCOMM Comput. Commun. Rev. 38(4), 15–26 (2008)
16. Khanna, A., Zinky, J.: The revised arpanet routing metric. SIGCOMM Comput. Commun. Rev. 19(4), 45–56 (1989)
17. Rétvári, G., Bíró, J.J., Cinkler, T.: On shortest path representation. IEEE/ACM Trans. Netw. 15(6), 1293–1306 (2007)
18. Thorup, M.: OSPF areas considered harmful. Internet Draft (April 2003)
19. Teixeira, R., Shaikh, A., Griffin, T., Rexford, J.: Dynamics of hot-potato routing in IP networks. SIGMETRICS Perform. Eval. Rev. 32(1), 307–319 (2004)

Intrinsic Monitoring Using Behaviour Models in IPv6 Networks

Edzard Höfig[1] and Hakan Coşkun[2,*]

[1] Fraunhofer Institute for Open Communication Systems, Berlin, Germany
`edzard.hoefig@fokus.fraunhofer.de`
[2] Faculty IV, Department of Design and Testing of Communication-Based Systems,
Technical University of Berlin, Germany
`coskun@cs.tu-berlin.de`

Abstract. In conventional networks, correlating path information to resource utilisation on the granularity of packets is a hard problem when using policy-based traffic handling schemes. We introduce a new approach
termed 'intrinsic monitoring' which relies on the use of IPv6 extension
headers in combination with formal behaviour models to gather resource
information along a path. This allows a network monitoring system to del-
egate monitoring functionality to the network devices themselves, with the
result of a drastic reduction in management traffic due to the increased autonomy of the monitoring system. As monitoring information travels in-
band with the network traffic, path information remains perfectly accurate.

Keywords: Intrinsic Monitoring, Network Management, IPv6, IPv6
Extension Headers, State Charts, Behaviour Model, Autonomic
Communication.

1 Introduction

From network planning to traffic engineering the visibility of the network state
with its corresponding resources is of crucial interest. If networks are equipped
with "intelligence", as it happens today, this becomes a challenging task. For instance, policy-based configuration is already used by network operators to better
utilise existing resources and to guarantee Quality-of-Service (QoS) constraints.If
an Internet Service Provider (ISP) puts mechanisms like policy routing in place,
it becomes possible to choose egress interfaces of routers depending on the destination addresses, port numbers, or application protocols of incoming packets.
Traffic coming from different applications on the same host can be assigned to
take different paths through the network, depending on protocol or traffic class.
By this, ISPs are allowed to change the network behaviour during runtime in
order to respond to new situations.

* The authors would like to acknowledge the European Commission for funding the
Integrated Project EFIPSANS "Exposing the Features in IP version Six protocols
that can be exploited/extended for the purposes of designing/building Autonomic
Networks and Services" within the 7th IST Framework Program.

J.C. Strassner and Y.M. Ghamri-Doudane (Eds.): MACE 2009, LNCS 5844, pp. 86–99, 2009.

In such a dynamic environment, traditional network measurement and monitoring can hardly provide a correct view of the utilised resources on a packet delivery path to a single destination. Today's networks already try to give capture network operation by employing technologies[1] to monitor attributes of network resources[2] and to use multi-point measurement architectures to track packets between any ingress and egress point of a domain [1]. Nevertheless, we still face a major problem: Correlating path information to resource utilisation on the granularity of packets. This is currently done off-line, in a centralised fashion, based on data acquired by several separate monitoring points spread throughout the network. Only an a posteriori reconstruction of the packet delivery path in combination with gathered resource utilisation data can reveal the desired information. Unfortunately, the more dynamic the traffic handling mechanisms, the higher the overhead for this process to yield accurate results. Hence, policy-based traffic handling poses a hard problem for conventional network monitoring approaches.

By exploiting new features of IPv6 in combination with ideas from the field of autonomic systems engineering we are able to show a simple, novel solution to this problem with far less monitoring traffic overhead than conventional approaches.

2   Intrinsic Monitoring on Network Routes

When observing the properties of network resources along an IPv6 network route within a certain domain in an on-demand manner, a typical setup like the one seen in Figure 1 is often used. Depicted is the path of packets that travel from a client to a server machine through the internet. One part of the route lies completely inside a single administrative domain, traffic entering the domain comes trough the Ingress router and leaves through the Egress router. To monitor information along a route inside the domain, a central management system needs first to conclude which routers are found on a packet's path by inspection of routing tables, or querying of topology databases, and subsequently poll every device using SNMP over a dedicated interface. Using such an approach is straightforward to implement and works with all but the most esoteric devices. Unfortunately, it exhibits a large overhead concerning the amount of SNMP packets that need to be transmitted for each observation. Scalability is also a major issue due to the centralised organisation of the monitoring management system.

In contrast, our approach, called 'intrinsic monitoring', introduces a new method to network monitoring and aims at solving these two issues. We do this by striving for two goals:

1. Reduction of monitoring and management traffic
2. Increased autonomy of the network monitoring system

The idea behind intrinsic monitoring is simple: We embed monitoring data within a suitable conventional packet and forward that packet along the route. Each

---

[1] Like Netflow, IPFIX, or SNMP.
[2] Like CPU utilisation, bandwidth, or packets counters.

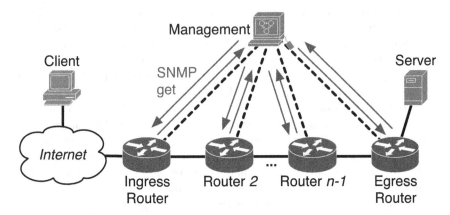

Fig. 1. Monitoring a route using SNMP polling

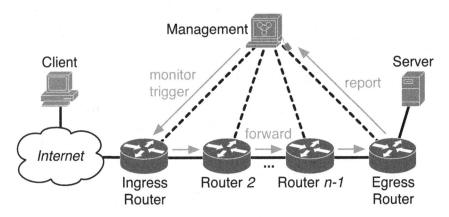

Fig. 2. Monitoring a route using intrinsic monitoring

device on the route updates the embedded information until the last router will report it back to the management system. From Figure 2 it is obvious that there will be a reduction in traffic. It can also be seen that routers need to be more autonomic: Router 2 ... Router n-1 are not directly communicating with the management system, they operate on their own accord.

We want to point out that we focus on a single domain rather than internet wide application of our approach. The reason behind this is simple, the control of network elements in a single domain is fully in the hand of the operator, giving him the freedom to apply new techniques (possibly proprietary) at any point in the network. Using new extension headers as we propose requires a standardization in advance. Otherwise, packets with unknown extensions are likely to be discarded.

To realise this scenario, we employ two novel mechanisms to the field of network monitoring: IPv6 extension headers and formalised behaviour models. Extension headers allow for the embedding of monitoring data in-band to the normal traffic and enable a distributed approach to monitoring management. Behaviour models can be used to formalise the operations that each router can apply on a packet. During runtime, models are executed to directly control a node's behaviour, yielding a flexible way to "teach" devices about the specific monitoring behaviours that they should execute on their own accord. This approach will only work if the necessary behaviour models are already deployed at the network devices prior to executing the monitoring task. Within this article we will not discuss how deployment is achieved, the reader can refer to a recent publication of us discussing deployment issues in more detail [2]. We assume that all necessary behaviour models already exist at the routers.

3   Behaviour Models: Teaching a Network Good Manners

A variety of instruments could potentially be used to specify behaviour models of nodes in packet-switching networks. Generally, every turing-complete formalism allowing for specification of discrete, reactive event systems could be employed (e.g. Petri-Nets or Automata). We choose to base our models on the visual State Chart formalism by Harel [3], which we also utilise to control device behaviour at runtime. State Charts are intuitively understood by humans, formally well defined, and widely used as part of UML 2. For this approach a certain overhead is necessary: the model needs to be interpreted at runtime and be given access to a state storage space and dynamic library bindings. These features provides us with the ability to teach specific monitoring behaviours to network devices without modification of statically bound code.

Let's have a look at some example behaviour models that demonstrate the use of intrinsic monitoring for collection of a single resource attribute value (e.g. CPU utilisation, dropped packets, temperature, etc.) from each router along a path. Figure 3 shows a behaviour model that queries a router for the current value of a resource attribute and subsequently updates an IPv6 extension header. The state-machine-like graphical notation shows three states connected by transitions. Transitions can be annotated with an event, a condition, and an action. In this case both events are specified as ε, defining that the transition is implicitly triggered, without an explicit event. There are no conditions used but two

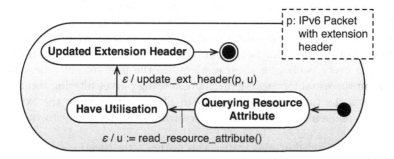

Fig. 3. Update of an extension header with resource attribute information

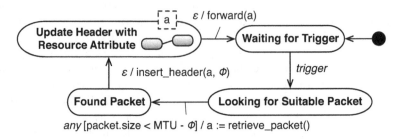

Fig. 4. Insertion of an extension header at ingress router

actions: read_resource_attribute() queries the router for the current value of the resource attribute via a dynamic library binding. We do not describe how such a functionality would be implemented at the router but assume that it should generally be possible using internal SNMP calls or by directly interfacing with the router operating system. The returned value is stored in the state storage space under the identifier u and thereafter used with the second action to update a packet's extension header. The packet that is being modified can be accessed using the identifier p, which has been handed to the model as a parameter. The usage of parameters has been introduced by us, whereas the notion of combined states[3] is already defined as part of the State Charts formalism.

Using the previously presented model for updating an extension header, we can now specify three behaviour models that together implement the intrinsic monitoring behaviour as seen in Figure 2. The first behaviour model waits for a trigger from the monitoring management system and subsequently looks for a packet that it can use to embedded the extension header in. Finding a suitable packet depends on the packet size: If we would attempt in-band monitoring in a naïve manner and simply attach a new extension header to an existing packet the packet size could easily grow larger than the path MTU (Maximum Transmission Unit), resulting in packet drop. We get around this problem by calculating the maximum extension header size Φ in advance using equation 1 in section 4.2 and then choosing a packet that can accommodate Φ bytes of additional data without invalidating the path MTU. Insertion of the extension header is done at the ingress router and follows the behaviour model shown in Figure 4.

Insertion of an intrinsic monitoring extension header is triggered by the management system through transmission of a *trigger* message that activates the first transition of the matching behaviour model at the ingress router. The router starts to scan every packet for its size, identifies the first suitable one, and removes it from the usual forwarding mechanism using packet filtering techniques. It then utilises the functionality depicted in Figure 3 to update the extension header before enqueuing the packet for forwarding and returning to the initial

---

[3] States can be embedded in other states. This feature is the basis for abstraction and distinguishes State Charts from conventional Finite State Machines. Another such feature is the ability to specify concurrent states.

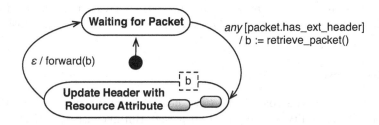

Fig. 5. Extension header modification at intermediary routers

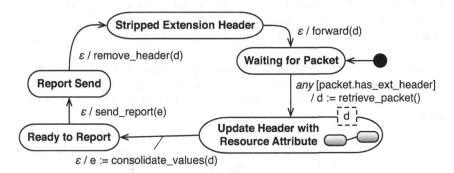

Fig. 6. Final report of monitoring data at egress router

behaviour state. From a functional point of view intermediary routers have a trivial task: they need to update any packet that arrives with an existing intrinsic monitoring extension header. Figure 5 shows how this is done, again relying on the previously mentioned "update header" composed state. This behaviour model is executed by all the intermediary routers on the path.

Last, but not least, the extension header needs to be removed from the inband traffic at the egress router, which is achieved by the specific behaviour model depicted in Figure 6. After retrieving an instrumented packet, the header is updated with the egress router's resource attribute value to complete the data acquisition, the data is afterwards consolidated in a report format and send with a report message to the management system. Subsequently the intrinsic monitoring header is removed from the packet and the packet forwarded to its actual destination.

4   Leveraging IPv6 Extension Headers

The rationale of our approach is to inject specific extension headers into the IPv6 data packets to collect and disseminate monitoring information that is related to different aspects of the communication. This gives us the opportunity to use already available data packets to disseminate monitoring data. This causes way more traffic in a network than necessary. But nevertheless, compared to traditional in-band monitoring we do not necessarily create new packets for the monitoring data, thus we reduce the overhead of monitoring traffic inside the network.

4.1 IPv6 Extension Headers

There is no doubt, the role of the IPv4 header is very important for the IP Protocol, this capability was kept in IPv6 as well. But in contrast to IPv4 packets which have only one header that includes addressing as well as options, the design of packets was changed in IPv6. The reason is due to the fact that routers have to parse each IPv4 header in order to process the options. This leads to performance loss during packet forwarding [4]. Taking this into consideration, the IETF came up with a new design that separate the options from the addressing and put them into additional headers. Therefore, IPv6 packets have a mandatory main header and the so called extension headers [5]. The mandatory header has a fixed size, whereas options are moved to extension headers that are attached to the packet when needed (see Figure 7). This separation reduces the cost of header processing significantly.

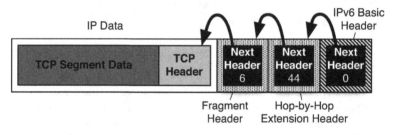

Fig. 7. IPv6 packet with chained extension headers

Unfortunately, the IETF missed to standardise a generic extension header format. As a result routers have to know each extension header in order to process it. Packets with unknown extension headers might be discarded, since the routers can not skip the unknown fields without knowing their size. A recently published internet draft proposes such a generic format [6] to solve this problem. In our work, we relate to this format and assume that future extension headers will follow this design.

4.2 MTU Imposes Maximum Extension Header Size

Fragmentation in IPv6 networks is only performed by source nodes. Injecting data into packets at intermediate nodes may pose a problem for the packet delivery. If IPv6 packets would grow with a fixed amount on a hop-by-hop basis, they could violate the path MTU. As a result, routers encountering such a problems would send ICMP Packet Too Big messages to the sources. Therefore, an extension header can only be used for information collection across the network when the creator pre-allocates enough space for the data to be inserted and still fit to the path MTU. The maximum size Φ depends on the number of routers M on the path, the size of data D to acquire on the route, and a constant given by the IPv6 extension header layout (we suppose 3 bytes). In the worst case M is the number of hops on the longest non-circular path within an administrative domain.

$$\Phi = M \times (16 + D) + 3 \qquad (1)$$

Φ is calculated in bytes and for our scenario we can set M to the number of routers on the single path that we consider. For example, the intrinsic monitoring extension header size for a maximum 4 hop route with collection of a single byte value for the resource attribute value per hop would be $4 \times 17 + 3 = 71$ bytes.

4.3   Resource Monitoring along Network Routes

One of the key benefits is that intrinsic monitoring allows us to collect information on the packet delivery path and to attach the monitoring data directly to the corresponding packets (see Figure 8). If intrinsic monitoring, as presented above, is supported by the router the interplay between header and state machine is sufficient to embed the requested resource attribute into the packet (context) it is related to. Thereby, obtaining resource attributes along a network path is not any more related to using inference mechanisms that analyze packet traces coming from multi-point measurements. For example, tracing routes for specific micro-flows can be realised by using only a few packets. Every trace will be triggered directly by the packet itself, there is no need to configure several measurement points to capture traffic with specific attributes or use multiple packets for each route as the classic traceroute application does. The route as a result will simply be stored in the header of each interested packet (micro-flow). Since, we consider a the usage of this monitoring scheme inside a single domain,

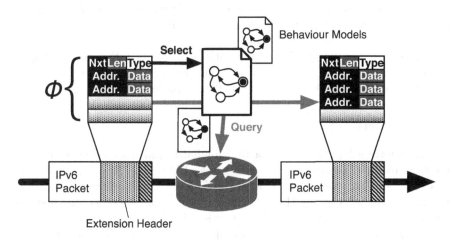

Fig. 8. Packet forwarding process using intrinsic monitoring

we can simply extract the extension header at the egress to report the path back to the sender or another network entity by embedding it into an ICMP message or just storing it into a IPFIX/Netflow records respectively. The latter is out of scope here and will be discussed in future work.

5   Related Work

5.1   In-band Monitoring

Real-time properties of network traffic are of crucial interest for several areas of networking. Capturing these properties incorporates monitoring and measurement techniques at different points in the network. Two types of approaches can be distinguished here, active and passive monitoring. Active monitoring injects additional packets into the network and follows them to measure the service obtained from the network. On the contrary, passive monitoring does not increase the network traffic, it observes and captures traffic that passes by. Both approaches are common in networking today. If the monitoring data follows the same paths as the traffic flows for users and applications, one refers to in-band monitoring. If paths are separated, monitoring is called out-of-band. According to that using IPv6 extension headers for network monitoring and measurement task is active in-band monitoring.

This is not a nouvel approach. IPv4 already had header options to collect information along a network path, called IP record route [7]. Although for IPv6 a similar approach was submitted to the IETF as drafts [8], it didnt make it. Nevertheless, the research community used the idea of collecting data along a network path by exploiting extension headers [9,10]. The advantage is obvious, monitoring data travels with the according packets. Usually, monitoring points (MP) have to be configure along the delivery path to perform the required metering/monitoring for the data flow [11]. In a big network, packets of a specific flow might take different paths, according to their type. This would lead to the a priori configuration of all monitoring points that will potentially "see" the packets.

Monitoring configured by hop-by-hop options might solve this. Monitoring is triggered by packets that carry intrinsic monitoring headers. There is no need to signal all potential MPs to observe specific micro-flows.

5.2   Statecharts

Statecharts have a long history as a tool for hard- and software specification, going back to the pioneering works of Mealy and Moore [12,13] and the formal works of Hoare [14], as well as Brand and Zafiropulo [15]. The concrete formalism has been invented by Harel to describe complex, reactive event systems [3]. It is often used at design time for functional requirements specification as part UML2 state diagrams, but also applied to the verification of functional behaviour [16,17], or employed for the visualisation of complex systems. More

recently, statecharts became popular as a specification technique for the generation of executable code as part of Model Driven Architecture (MDA) processes
[18,19]. It has also been shown that statecharts can be executed [20], for example
to simulate system behaviour. Currently, researchers are exploring options for
execution of state machines at run-time. The most visible effort towards this
direction is the specification of SCXML: a XML based language for description
of statecharts [21], along with matching runtime environments.

6   Conclusion

6.1   Packet Transmission Overhead

We will now compare the packet transmission overhead of resource attribute
acquisition on a route consisting of N routers and ignoring packet loss. For the
SNMP case one needs $2N$ packet transmissions as every node is polled individually. For intrinsic monitoring we need to consider the packet that is transmitted
between each intermediary router on the path plus the trigger message and the
additional report packet at the egress point, resulting in an overall $N + 1$ packet
transmissions. This shows that packet transmission overhead for the SNMP scenario is nearly twice as high as for the intrinsic monitoring case. To discuss the
management traffic overhead of our approach we define a criterion called the
'autonomy level'.

Definition of the Autonomy Level. We define the autonomy level based on
the ratio between the number of monitoring packets transmitted on the management network P_c and the overall number of monitoring packets P.

$$\alpha = 1 - \frac{P_c}{P} \tag{2}$$

Calculation of α for the SNMP case is trivial: $P = P_c = 2N$, as all of the
monitoring packets are relayed using management network links. This gives us
an autonomy level of $\alpha = 0$. For the intrinsic monitoring case $P = N + 1$ and
the number of control packets is constant $P_c = 2$. This leads to the definition of
the autonomy level for intrinsic monitoring systems as

$$\alpha = 1 - \frac{2}{N + 1} \tag{3}$$

Figure 9 shows how α changes with a growing number of routers. The system
behaves more autonomic the more devices exist on the monitored route. This
demonstrates that intrinsic monitoring pays off in terms of management effort
reduction when implemented on even the smallest route between two hosts, but
also shows the approach has more benefits the larger the network is.

Our definition of autonomy has been influenced by Holzer, et al. who define
autonomy based on the ratio between the entropy of control information and
overall system information [22]. For a study of the packet overhead of the scenario

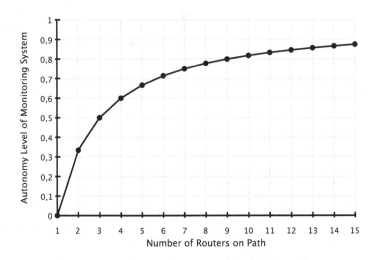

Fig. 9. Intrinsic monitoring system autonomy level vs. number of routers on path

our definition is sufficient, but we are also aware that there are problems with it. For example our definition does not allow us to compare different systems purely on the grounds of their autonomy levels. A possible remedy (e.g. for data-intensive scenarios) might be to also take the information entropy in account as done in the original definition, which would allow for differentiation of messages according to the uniqueness of their content.

6.2   Packet Processing Overhead

IPv6 was designed to require less processing overhead. Fragmentation was left out, checksums do not exist any more, all extension headers except the hop-by-hop options header are analysed by the destination node. The overhead to insert arbitrary information into the header stems from the fact, that every packet that has an according pre-allocated intrinsic monitoring header has to be parsed by the router. This always means that packets have to go through the slow path processing, which again reduces the performance of the router. But this problem not related to our approach, it is inherent to IPv6. For instance, the presence of an IPv6 Router Alert Option [23] inside a packet causes it to traverse the slow path of the router, as well.

The additional overhead for interpretation of behaviour models at network devices is hard to quantify due to the wide variety that potential behaviour models can exhibit. In general, we can differentiate two main functionalities that allot processing time: The behaviour model interpreting mechanism ('interpreter overhead'), and the resource attribute query actions executed within a device ('action overhead'). When querying a resource attribute using SNMP the same action overhead is caused as if the query would be triggered through the behaviour model, we therefore can exclude the action overhead from the discussion. The story is different for the interpreter overhead. The overhead depends largely on the structure of a given behaviour model, but we found during prior work on efficient state machine interpreters [24] that the main overhead lies in the selection of the active transition, the evaluation of conditional expressions, and the internal event handling. Compared to other approaches (e.g. fact-based reasoning engines, script execution) state machine based interpretation can be regarded as a low-level mechanism that is fast to execute. We expect to be in the same performance class as other approaches that rely on the processing of hop-by-hop extension headers, as long as the attributes that can be put into the packets do not require extensive calculation.

6.3 Open Issues and Outlook

Dimensioning the Pre-allocation Size Φ. Setting the intrinsic monitoring extension header to a size big enough that it can hold all entries for the potentially longest possible route in a domain (see section 4.2) seems to be an unsatisfactory solution. A dynamic Φ that would be adopted to a given path MTU, for example during the path MTU discovery process for IPv6 [25], would be a cleaner solution but could also collide with dynamic traffic handling schemes. It would also be necessary to test if real-world IPv6 implementations can cope with dynamically growing packets and to study any dependencies that this might have with other protocol features (e.g. checksum calculation for authentication purposes). Another problem arises from the fact that IPv6 supports fragmentation at the sender. Until now, we assumed that packets are not fragmented, but tracing packet delivery, requires to cope with packet fragmentation. In future we will look at this feature.

Performance of Packet Filtering. For our approach to work, a router needs to be capable of checking every single packet for certain properties. In our example there are only two properties: the existence of the intrinsic monitoring extension header and the packet size (see section 3), but generally these properties would depend on the functionality of the monitoring process and its specification through the behaviour models. We suspect that most IPv6 capable routers would be able to filter packets according to a wide sets of criteria at wire-speed, but we did not research this yet. Additionally, the routers would need to not only be able to filter a packet, but also to dequeue it from the forwarding mechanism and to later enqueue a modified packet. Currently, we are studying the minimal runtime requirements and performance overhead for execution of behaviour models in detail using an implementation on a resource-constrained platform[4]. First results look promising: they show feasibility of the approach and an existing, but bound performance overhead.

We have already performed a simulative study of our presented approach using the network simulator OMNeT++ to investigate its feasibility [26]. The results are promising. They indicate that our approach seems to be realizable in real networks. Of course, we are aware of the gap between simulations and real

---

[4] 8 bit microcontroller, 2 KByte RAM, 16 MHz core frequency.

world networks, due to the lack of features supported by simulators. To study the intrinsic monitoring approach inside real IPv6 networks, we are currently implementing a prototype of the presented work in the context of the European project EFIPSANS.

References

1. Duffield, N.G., Grossglauser, M.: Trajectory sampling for direct traffic observation. SIGCOMM Comput. Commun. Rev. 30(4), 271–282 (2000)
2. Höfig, E., Deussen, P.H.: Document-based network and system management: utilizing autonomic capabilities for enterprise management integration. In: Proc. 2nd International Conference on Autonomic Computing and Communication Systems, pp. 1–10 (2008)
3. Harel, D.: Statecharts: A visual formalism for complex systems. Science of Computer Programming 8(3), 231–274 (1987)
4. Moestedt, A., Sjödin, P., Köhler, T.: Header processing requirements and implementation complexity for ipv4 routers. White Paper (September 1998)
5. Deering, S., Hinden, R.: Internet Protocol, Version 6 (IPv6) Specification. RFC 2460 (Draft Standard), Updated by RFC 5095 (December 1998)
6. Krishnan, S., Woodyatt, J., Kline, E., Hoagland, J.: An uniform format for IPv6 extension headers. Internet-Draft draft-krishnan-ipv6-exthdr-06, Internet Engineering Task Force, Work in progress (October 2008)
7. Postel, J.: RFC 791: Internet Protocol (September 1981)
8. Kitamura, H.: Record Route for IPv6 (RR6) Hop-by-Hop Option Extension. Internet-Draft draft-kitamura-ipv6-record-route-00, Internet Engineering Task Force, Work in progress (November 2000)
9. Pezaros, D., Hutchison, D., Sventek, J., Garcia, F., Gardner, R.: In-line service measurements: an ipv6-based framework for traffic evaluation and network operations. In: Network Operations and Management Symposium, NOMS 2004, April 2004, vol. 1, pp. 497–510. IEEE/IFIP (2004)
10. Pezaros, D., Sifalakis, M., Schmid, S., Hutchison, D.: Dynamic link measurements using active components. In: Minden, G.J., Calvert, K.L., Solarski, M., Yamamoto, M. (eds.) Active Networks. LNCS, vol. 3912, pp. 188–204. Springer, Heidelberg (2007)
11. Hancock, R., Karagiannis, G., Loughney, J., den Bosch, S.V.: Next Steps in Signaling (NSIS): Framework. RFC 4080 (Informational) (June 2005)
12. Moore, E.: Gedanken-experiments on sequential machines. Automata studies 34, 129–153 (1956)
13. Mealy, G.: A method for synthesizing sequential circuits. Bell System Technical Journal 34(5), 1045–1079 (1955)
14. Hoare, C.A.: Communicating sequential processes. Communications of the ACM (January 1978)
15. Brand, D., Zafiropulo, P.: On communicating finite-state machines. Journal of the Association for Computing Machinery 30(2), 323–342 (1983)
16. Dong, W., Wang, J., Qi, X., Qi, Z.: Model checking UML statecharts. In: Eighth Asia-Pacific on Software Engineering Conference, APSEC 2001, pp. 363–370 (2001)
17. Latella, D., Majzik, I., Massink, M.: Automatic verification of a behavioural subset of UML statechart diagrams using the SPIN model-checker. Formal Aspects of Computing 11(6), 637–664 (1999)

18. Knapp, A., Merz, S.: Model checking and code generation for UML state machines and collaborations. In: Proceedings of 5th Workshop on Tools for System Design and Verification, Technical Report, vol. 11, pp. 59–64 (2002)
19. Niaz, I., Tanaka, J.: Code generation from UML statecharts. In: Proc. 7 th IASTED International Conf. on Software Engineering and Application (SEA 2003), pp. 315–321 (2003)
20. Harel, D., Gery, E.: Executable object modeling with statecharts. In: Proceedings of the 18th International Conference on Software Engineering, 1996, pp. 246–257 (1996)
21. World Wide Web Consortium: State Chart XML (SCXML): State machine notation for control abstraction (May 2009)
22. Holzer, R., Meer, H., Bettstetter, C.: On autonomy and emergence in self-organizing systems. In: Hummel, K.A., Sterbenz, J.P.G. (eds.) IWSOS 2008. LNCS, vol. 5343, pp. 157–169. Springer, Heidelberg (2008)
23. Partridge, C., Jackson, A.: IPv6 router alert option. RFC 2711, Internet Engineering Task Force (October 1999)
24. Hinnerichs, A., Höfig, E.: An efficient mechanism for matching multiple patterns on XML streams. In: Proc. of the IASTED Int. Conf. on Software Engineering, pp. 164–170 (2007)
25. McCann, J., Deering, S., Mogul, J.: Path MTU Discovery for IP version 6. RFC 1981 (Draft Standard) (August 1996)
26. Omnet++ discrete event simulation system, http://www.omnetpp.org

Utilization of a Cooperative Multiagent System in the Context of Cognitive Radio Networks

Usama Mir, Leila Merghem-Boulahia, and Dominique Gaïti

ICD/ERA, FRE CNRS 2848, Université de Technologie de Troyes, 12 rue Marie Curie,
10010 Troyes Cedex, France
{usama.mir,leila.merghem_boulahia,dominique.gaiti}@utt.fr

Abstract. In this paper we propose an approach to solve the spectrum alloca-
tion/sharing problem using Multiagent System (MAS) cooperation that enables
Cognitive Radio (CR) devices to share the unutilized spectrum dynamically and
opportunistically. We introduce briefly the problem of static spectrum assignment and propose an approach to solve this issue. The key aspect of our design
is the deployment of agents on each of the CR and Primary User (PU) devices
that cooperate in order to have a better use of the spectrum. An example scenario is also presented along with our proposed model.

Keywords: Multiagent Systems, Cognitive Radios, Dynamic Spectrum Shar-
ing/allocation, Cooperation.

1 Introduction

According to a recent study by the Federal Communications Commission (FCC), in
all the areas (either rural or urban), spectrum use is static and could thus be wasteful
[2]. Cognitive radio (CR) [8] is considered to be a growing phenomenon in modern
wireless systems to solve this static spectrum assignment problem. In general, a CR
node works opportunistically as to first detect the empty *spectrum holes* [2] and later
to share these *holes* dynamically, in order to avoid the interference with the other
licensed or unlicensed users. To achieve efficient and dynamic allocation of spectrum
between highly distributed CR devices, a balanced, simple and cooperative approach
is necessary [1]. Research is therefore in progress on understanding the cooperative
sharing techniques in Cognitive Radio Networks (CRNs). On the other hand, a Multi-
agent System (MAS) [6] is composed of multiple autonomous and intelligent agents,
working individually or in groups (through interaction) to solve particular tasks. Like
CR nodes, agents also work dynamically to fulfill their user needs and no single agent
has a global view of the network. The novelty of our work is the development of a
model that allows us to allocate spectrum dynamically and in a collaborative manner
by combining both the functionalities of CR devices and MAS. The cooperation
mechanism of proposed approach is similar to that of Contract Net Protocol (CNP)
[9]. The paper is organized as follows: In section 2, we present a state of the art review of related approaches. Section 3 explains our context with the help of a scenario.
In Section 4, we propose our model with the interlinked working of various modules
and section 5 delineates the future work and the conclusion.

J.C. Strassner and Y.M. Ghamri-Doudane (Eds.): MACE 2009, LNCS 5844, pp. 100–104, 2009.
© Springer-Verlag Berlin Heidelberg 2009

2 Related Work

The spectrum sharing has recently attracted the research attention especially using game-theoretical approaches [3], but there is not much work done for the utilization of cooperative MAS in CRNs. A related approach is proposed in [1], in which MAS is used for information sharing and spectrum assignments. All the participating agents deployed over Access Points (APs), form an interacting MAS, which is responsible for managing radio resources across collocated WLANs. Further the authors have presented each agent's architecture, which consists of two main parts including *Predictive Parameter Estimation (PPE)* (responsible for generating parameters estimates using the signal characteristics received from WLAN environment). *PPE*'s parameters are then served as an input to architecture's second part named as *resource management optimization*. *Resource management optimization* is responsible for making the main decisions of AP including; which request is to be accepted from Mobile Stations (MSs), transmit power control and less interfered channel selection. The authors have not provided any of the algorithms and results for their approach.

In [4], another MAS based approach is presented, where a distributed and dynamic billing, pricing and resource allocation mechanism is proposed. The protocol used for radio resource allocation between the CR devices and operators is termed as *multiunit sealed-bid auction*, which is based on the concept of bidding and assigning resources. The agents work as the *auctioneers* and the *bidders* to share the spectrum dynamically. The whole environment architecture consists of several parts including *QoS Buffer Management (QoS-BM)* (determines the data to be sent first), *User Profile Manager (UPM)* (identifies the QoS requirements and spectrum preferences of the CR users) and *Bidding Strategy (BIS)* (gets its input from *QoS-BM* to make a resource requesting bid). The authors have given a complete statistical analysis of the approach with the calculation of CR user's utility, input strategy, cost, etc, but still the whole system is really complex, including the complexity in time required to calculate the optimal spectrum allocation.

3 A Scenario for Cooperative Spectrum Sharing

The proposed scenario addresses the spectrum allocation challenges in a private area or a well identified administrated perimeter such as a campus, an airport, a conference center or a hospital. There are different ad-hoc WLANs deployed in the area with sets of primary (licensed) and secondary (cognitive or unlicensed) users. For the purpose of cooperation between the devices, agents are deployed at each of them (fig. 1). Whenever a CR device detects an empty portion of the spectrum as needed by its user, its agent starts communicating with the relative primary user agent (having that empty spectrum part), until a spectrum sharing agreement is been made.

An application domain of this scenario can be a hospital. In this context, many technologies are used at the same time (GSM, WiMax) and the number of users cannot be determined in a precise way. With CR, a given terminal (a doctor's PDA, an RFID bracelet of a patient, a camera transmitting a chirurgical intervention) will be

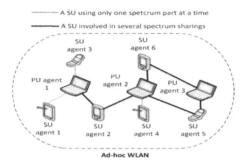

Fig. 1. Various ad-hoc WLANs having different sets of primary and CR users with the agents deployed on them

able to choose the best spectrum band/channel. This choice is made in cooperation with the other agents embarked on the PU devices, by taking into account the amount of spectrum needed, the respected time limit and the related price [10].

4 Proposed Approach

Our secondary user based design (fig. 2) consists of several parts. Firstly, the **Dynamic Spectrum Sensor (DSS)** works as to sense *spectrum holes* or *white spaces*. There are many techniques available for spectrum sensing such as PU's weak signal and its energy detection while mixing it with oscillatory signals [2] and cooperative centralized detection [5]. The second part is **Spectrum Characterizer (SC)**[1] which characterizes each spectrum portion (with relative PU) in terms of *capacity* (the amount of total unused spectrum of a PU) using Shannon's capacity estimation theorem [7]. **Secondary User Interface (SUI)** is the third part that sends a QoS message to the SU device agent whenever a user wants to have a portion of spectrum (for video conferencing, watching high quality videos).

Our fourth design part is **Agent's Knowledge Module (AKM)** which creates a *capacity* based descending order list of related[2] PUs, based on the characterization results received through SC module. This list is sent to the next module and it is also updated whenever CR senses another empty spectrum portion. Based on inputs from SC and SUI modules, AKM prepares a *Call for Proposal (CfP)* message such as:

$$CfP\ (SUID,\ s,\ t,\ p,\ d)$$

Where '*SUID*' is the secondary user agent's identification and it is used to help PU to reply back to the same requested SU, '*s*' is the amount of spectrum requested by the SU, '*t*' refers to the respected time limit (or holding time) for the spectrum utilization based on SU's QoS requirements, '*p*' is the price SU is willing to pay based on its spectrum usage and '*d*' is the deadline to receive the PUs' responses (proposals).

---

[1] The main focus of our work is on the second part of fig. 2, i.e. the agent module.

[2] If an SU needs 8MB of spectrum, then by looking at the capacity-based list, the SU only sends messages to those PU agent(s) who have either 8MB or more free spectrum portions.

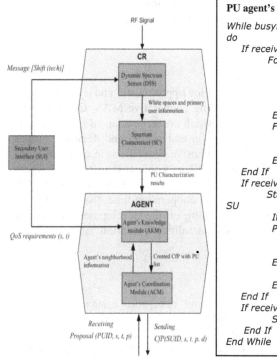

Fig. 2. Internal architecture of SU

PU agent's Proposal Creation and Submission

While busyflag = false
do
   If received message = CfP
     For each received CfP do
      Characterize CfP using $\dfrac{p(n)}{s(n) \times t(n)}$
      and add it in L(n)
     End For
     For best CfP in L(n) do
      Construct a proposal (PUID,s,t,p)
      and send it to corresponding SU
     End For
   End If
   If received message = accept
     Start spectrum sharing with selected SU
     If still some other unused spectrum
     Parts are available
      Continue analyzing further
      CfPs for spectrum sharing
     Else
      Set busyflag = true
     End If
   End If
   If received message = reject
     Start reanalyzing further CfP(s)
   End If
End While

Fig. 3. Behavior of PU agent

The last part **Agent Coordination Module (ACM)** is responsible for managing the inter–agent communications. After the reception of *CfP* message from AKM, ACM examines the message based on its neighborhood knowledge and PU characterization list in order to choose a suitable PU agent. In a positive case, it geo-casts the *CfP* to the available addresses, otherwise it waits for any of its neighboring PUs to send their *proposals*[3]. The fetched *proposal(s)* from PU(s) are locally sorted and an *accept* message is sent to a selected PU agent by looking at the amount of spectrum it is willing to give with the associated *holding time* and *price*. The information of selected PU is also sent to AKM for future cooperations. When SU has only one *proposal* in its cache and it satisfies SU requirements, an *accept* message is directly sent to the corresponding PU, otherwise if still there is no *proposal* received until the deadline expiration, SU recreates and resends its *CfP* with a modified value of *price*. This value can attract several other PUs and there exists a relatively higher chance that they will submit their *proposals* to the modified *CfP*.

In some situations, normally SU wants another portion of the spectrum after completely utilizing the currently assigned one. Thus, by looking at the PUs list maintained by AKM in its local cache, the spectrum sharing can be directly started by

---

[3] The *proposal* creation mechanism, working and internal behaviour of PU can be understood by looking at fig. 3.

sending messages (such as *CfP, proposal, accept*) to any of the specific eligible PU(s). This process will reduce the message geo-casting overhead.

5 Conclusion

In this paper, we have presented a design model for opportunistic and dynamic spectrum sharing and allocation in CR networks using cooperative MAS. Currently, we are working on several cooperative algorithms which are to be adapted in the context of CR networks. Later, we will be considering on elaborating and detailing further scenarios. In the continuing work, we will run extensive simulations in order to evaluate our proposed algorithms. The simulations will be conducted using Java Agent Development Framework (JADE) by considering several parameters such as the CR user's utility, number of exchanged messages, the cooperation time, the related spectrum price, etc. In future, we will also be working on the development of various spectrum sharing algorithms using the methods of coalition formation.

References

1. Jiang, X., Ivan, H., Anita, R.: Cognitive radio resource management using multi-agent systems. In: Consumer communications and networking conference, CCNC, pp. 1123–1127. IEEE Communication Society, Las Vegas (2007)
2. Akyildiz, F., Lee, W.-Y., Vuran, M.C., Mohanty, S.: NeXt generation/dynamic spectrum access/cognitive radio wireless networks: A survey. International Journal of computer and telecommunications networking, 2127–2159 (2006)
3. James: O'Neel. In: Analysis and design of cognitive radio networks and distributed radio resource management algorithms. ACM press, Virginia (2006)
4. Kloeck, H.J., Jondra, F.: Multi-agent radio resource allocation. In: Mobile Networks and Applications, MONET, pp. 813–824. ACM, Amsterdam (2006)
5. Wild, B., Ramchandran, K.: Detecting primary receivers for cognitive radio applications. In: IEEE Dynamic Spectrum Access Networks, DySPAN, pp. 124–130. IEEE Press, Piscataway (2005)
6. Panait, L., LukeOn, S.: Cooperative multi-agent systems learning: state of the art. In: Autonomous Agents and Multi-Agent Systems, AAMAS, pp. 387–434. ACM, New York (2005)
7. Dimitrakopoulos, G., Demestichas, P., Grandblaise, D., Mößner, K., Hoffmeyer, J., Luo, J.: Cognitive radio, spectrum and radio resource management. In: Wireless World Research Forum, WWRF, London (2004)
8. Mitola, J.: Cognitive radio: an integrated agent architecture for software defined radio, Ph.D Thesis, KTH Royal Institute of Technology, Kista (2000)
9. Smith, R.G.: The contract net protocol: high-level communication and control in a distributed problem solver. In: Distributed Artificial Intelligence Book, pp. 357–366. Morgan Kaufmann Publishers Inc., San Francisco (1981)
10. TEROPP,
    http://era.utt.fr/fr/projets_de_recherche/carnot_teropp.html

On the Design of an Architecture for Partitioned Knowledge Management in Autonomic Multimedia Access and Aggregation Networks

Steven Latré, Stijn Verstichel, Bart De Vleeschauwer,
Filip De Turck, and Piet Demeester

IBCN, Department of Information Technology, Ghent University - IBBT
Gaston Crommenlaan 8/201, 9050 Gent, Belgium
Steven.Latre@intec.ugent.be

Abstract. The recent emergence of multimedia services, such as Network Based Personal Video Recording and Broadcast TV over traditional DSL based access networks, has introduced stringent Quality of Experience (QoE) requirements. It is generally assumed that the wide variety of services and user profiles introduces the need for a per-user or per-subscriber QoE management. Such a complex QoE management requires real-time knowledge about the managed services, which is available amongst the different nodes in the network. However, even for managing a few services, a relatively large amount of, constantly updated, knowledge is needed. Propagating all the knowledge to all nodes is therefore not feasible. As not all knowledge is relevant to all nodes, it is important to perform an intelligent knowledge distribution and management. In this position paper, we introduce the concept of a cognitive model that describes the knowledge requirements of each node. Based on the information stated in this cognitive model, we discuss how filter queries, that typically describe what needs to be queried from other nodes, can be automatically generated leading to an efficient partitioning of the knowledge through the distributed nodes.

1 Introduction

Multimedia services over broadband DSL access and aggregation networks such as Broadcast TV and Video on Demand have gained a lot of popularity in the last few years. For end users, these services introduce new possibilities such as interactivity and higher video quality. For service operators, multimedia services offer an increased revenue in their Triple Play offer. At the same time, these multimedia services have stringent quality requirements: they often require a substantial amount of bandwidth and tolerate no packet loss and only small amounts of jitter. Operators who want to maximise their revenue try to manage the service quality as perceived by the end user, commonly described as the Quality of Experience (QoE). This QoE management is further complicated by the heterogeneity of today's access and aggregation networks. A wide variety of service enablers such as proxies, caches, admission control techniques and

J.C. Strassner and Y.M. Ghamri-Doudane (Eds.): MACE 2009, LNCS 5844, pp. 105–110, 2009.

transcoders that are able to modify the QoE of services exist, but the challenge lies in the activation and configuration of these service enablers, in such a way that the QoE of individual services is maximised and the quality of existing services is protected.

The huge amount of services and the wide variety of service enablers and user profiles call for a QoE management on a per service or per subscriber basis. Such a fine grained QoE management introduces the need for detailed knowledge about users and services. As an autonomic network management architecture is by definition distributed, the knowledge available in one node can also be of interest for other nodes to help in their reasoning process. However, it is not possible to flood all nodes with all knowledge available as this would lead to an explosion of the amount of knowledge in every node. Furthermore, as only part of the knowledge might be of interest to other nodes, the bulk of monitor information should not be forwarded to other nodes as it is not of any relevance. The challenge lies in dynamically selecting which knowledge should be made available to which nodes.

The contributions of this paper are two-fold. First, we introduce the concept of a cognitive model to a Knowledge Based Network (KBN) architecture that provides information about the reasoning process in the autonomic control loop. The cognitive model allows for defining the knowledge requirements of each node in a structured and coherent way. Second, we describe how the cognitive model can be used to automatically generate filter queries, which defines the information that needs to be requested from other nodes.

The remainder of this paper is structured as follows. In the next section, we elaborate on relevant work in the domain of autonomic network management and the link with KBNs. Section 3 discusses the integration of the cognitive model within the KBN architecture. Finally, in Section 4, the automatic generation of filter queries based on information in the cognitive model is discussed for the employed implementation.

2   Related Work

The complex management of today's networks has triggered the research for autonomic communications, where the network is able to govern itself. Recently, several autonomic architectures have been proposed such as the FOCALE [1] architecture, which focuses on the heterogeneity of distributed resources, and the KPlane [2] architecture which applies the Knowledge Plane paradigm, as originally proposed by Clark [3], to optimise the QoE in access and aggregation networks. Both architectures advocate the need for an information model as the basis for an autonomic network control loop [4,5].

The problem of organising knowledge in an autonomic network has been addressed through the Knowledge Based Network paradigm [6,7]. In a Knowledge Based Network, producers of information describe the available information through ontologies. Consumers subscribe to this information through semantic queries. The work presented in this paper complements this approach: while the

KBN work focuses on semantic clustering of information [8] and augmenting the semantic capabilities of existing solutions [9], we focus on the automatic generation of the semantic queries, which we call filter queries, through a cognitive model.

3   Architecture Description

An overview of the employed architecture, which is responsible for collecting the necessary knowledge for each node by querying information present in other remote nodes, is given in Figure 1. The architecture consists of three main components: (1) the information model, holding all relevant knowledge for performing the reasoning, (2) the cognitive model, holding information about the reasoning process and its knowledge requirements, and (3) the knowledge partitioner, responsible for automatically generating filter queries. These three components are discussed in the remainder of this section.

Information model. At the heart of the architecture lies the information model which represents all knowledge needed for the higher layer functions. Conceptually, the architecture splits the information model of every node into different sub models. Every node X has a dedicated information model and several derived information models, containing parts of the information model of other (e.g. neighbouring) nodes. The dedicated information model consists of knowledge which is local to node X. In practice this will be locally obtained monitor information or the outcome of locally performed reasoning decisions. The derived information models contain parts of the information models of other nodes and typically contain knowledge which can aid in the reasoning process of node X such as monitor information of a service running through node X (e.g. the suffered packet loss ratio of a video session further down the path) or decisions

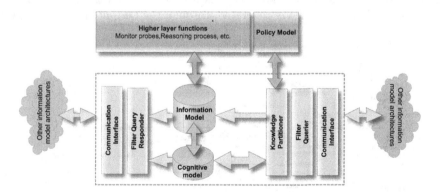

Fig. 1. Architecture for effective knowledge communication in autonomic multimedia access and aggregation networks. Use case specific queries, that enable to filter the requested knowledge, are automatically derived based on stated policies and a cognitive model.

made by reasoning processes on other nodes. The derived models are constructed through filter queries, defining which part of the knowledge is requested from other nodes.

Cognitive model. The cognitive model comprises information about the capabilities of each node and describes which kind of knowledge is generated by each node. Additionally, the cognitive model provides information about the requirements of the local reasoning process by stating what kind of information is needed to reason upon. If the reasoning process is formalised (e.g. through a formal language), the selection can be done automatically, otherwise, the information needs to be specified.

Knowledge Partitioner. The information available in the cognitive model is used to select the data that needs to be extracted from other information models. This is done in the Knowledge Partitioner, a third component in the architecture. For each node, the Knowledge Partitioner selects which information from that remote node is needed by the local node. The information extracted from the remote node must aid in the reasoning process of the local node.

4   Automatic Generation of Filter Queries

The architecture discussed in Section 3 foresees in the automatic generation of filter queries through the Knowledge Partitioner. To automatically generate the necessary queries, the Knowledge Partitioner relies on knowledge about the reasoning process defined through the cognitive model. The cognitive model used in our implementation, which is tightly coupled with the employed information model as described in [5], is illustrated in Figure 2. The illustrated concepts can be divided into three groups. A first group (a), provides information about the reasoning process itself. The cognitive model describes how reasoning is performed on this node and what knowledge is needed, through the *InputClause* concept, and what knowledge is generated, through the *OutputClause* concept.

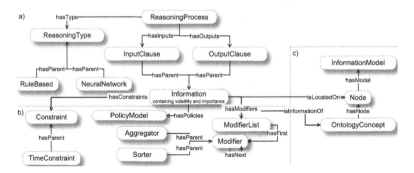

Fig. 2. Schematic overview of the concepts and relationships introduced in the cognitive model. The cognitive model provides information about the (a) reasoning process, (b) knowledge needed and (c) availability of remote knowledge.

In the *Information* concept the volatility, describing how frequently the information needs to be refreshed, and importance, describing if the information is strictly needed or not, of the information is defined. In the second group (b), the cognitive model describes how this information is treated by the reasoning process. The cognitive model supports that information can be modified (e.g. aggregating and sorting) or the results being filtered through constraints. Furthermore, the requested information has a link with the *PolicyModel* concept. Through this link, decisions can be made whether or not to retrieve the requested information based on the volatility and importance properties and the corresponding policy rules. For example, in some cases a reasoning process does not need all information to make an accurate decision. In that case, information can be marked by the cognitive model as less important. While, the reasoning process still requests this information through the cognitive model, depending on the used policy rules, the policy model can decide to ignore this request to avoid a high communication overhead. The third part of the cognitive model (c) describes which concepts are modelled on remote information models. This information is needed to know where the filter queries need to be redirected to and if the requested knowledge is available or not.

The knowledge available in the cognitive model can be easily added by investigating the reasoning process of each entity. The Knowledge Partitioner studies the reasoning process and determines the minimum knowledge needed by limiting the requested information through modifiers and constraints. For example, for a rule based engine, the facts needed to trigger rules can be seen as the *InputClauses* of the cognitive model. Depending on how this information occurs in the rules, they may or may not be aggregated. Furthermore, information about the *OntologyConcepts* and their location can be deducted based on the generated information. In our implementation, the majority of information is automatically derived through ontology reasoning.

Based on this cognitive model, constructing the filter queries is straightforward. Each individual of the *InputClause* concept is mapped to a basic, atomic, filter query that needs to be executed. Through the is *isLocatedOn* and *hasModel* relationships the Knowledge Partitioner knows which information model to contact. Additional modifiers and constraints can be directly applied to the filter queries by investigating the corresponding relationships. In our implementation we support basic modifiers and constraints such as calculating an average or filtering values through comparison. Note that these modifiers and constraints are also available in common query languages such as SQL and the ontology query language SPAQRL [10]. When all basic filter queries are generated, they are grouped by the node they need to be requested from. Optionally, these groups of queries can be optimised to to avoid requesting for the same information twice.

5   Conclusions and Future Work

We discussed how filter queries in Knowledge Based Networks can be automatically generated through the use of a cognitive model. The cognitive model, which is closely linked with an information model, defines the knowledge requirements of each node by identifying the reasoning processes running on each node and describing the information they need to perform their task. The structure of the cognitive model allows to easily map the information onto filter queries. These filter queries define which knowledge needs to be transferred and in what form.

In future work, we are targeting to evaluate the architecture by linking it with information models of different complexity to investigate the scalability of the approach. Furthermore, we plan to investigate the use of more formal reasoning processes, for example through the use of a formal language to describe the reasoning or by exploiting the use of ontologies, to further automate the generation of the cognitive model, resulting in a semi-automated conversion from reasoning process to cognitive model.

References

1. Strassner, J., Agoulmine, N., Lehtihet, E.: Focale a novel autonomic networking architecture. In: Latin American Autonomic Computing Symposium (LAACS) (July 18-19)
2. Latré, S., Simoens, P., De Vleeschauwer, B., Van de Meerssche, W., De Turck, F., Dhoedt, B., Demeester, P., Van den Berghe, S., Gilon de Lumley, E.: An autonomic architecture for optimizing QoE in multimedia access networks. Computer Networks 53(10), 1587–1602 (2009)
3. Clark, D.D., Partridge, C., Ramming, J.C., Wroclawski, J.T.: A knowledge plane for the internet. In: SIGCOMM 2003: Proceedings of the 2003 conference on Applications, technologies, architectures, and protocols for computer communications, pp. 3–10. ACM Press, New York (2003)
4. Strassner, J.: Den-ng: achieving business-driven network management. In: Network Operations and Management Symposium, NOMS 2002, pp. 753–766. IEEE/IFIP (2002)
5. Latré, S., Simoens, P., De Vleeschauwer, B., Van de Meerssche, W., De Turck, F., Dhoedt, B., Demeester, P., Van den Berghe, S., Gilon de Lumley, E.: Design of a generic knowledge base for autonomic QoE optimization in multimedia access networks. In: ACNM 2008: 2nd IEEE Workshop on Autonomic Communications for Network Management (2008)
6. Lewis, D., O' Sullivan, D., Keeney, J.: Towards the knowledge-driven benchmarking of autonomic communications. In: International Symposium on a World of Wireless, Mobile and Multimedia Networks, WoWMoM 2006, pp. 500–505 (2006)
7. Lewis, D., O'sullivan, D., Feeney, K., Keeney, J., Power, R.: Ontology-based engineering for self-managing communications. In: Workshop on Modelling Autonomic Communications Environments (2006)
8. Keeney, J., Jones, D., Roblek, D., Lewis, D., O'Sullivan, D.: Knowledge-based semantic clustering. In: SAC 2008: Proceedings of the 2008 ACM symposium on Applied computing, pp. 460–467. ACM Press, New York (2008)
9. Keeney, J., Roblek, D., Jones, D., Lewis, D., O'Sullivan, D.: Extending siena to support more expressive and flexible subscriptions. In: DEBS 2008: Proceedings of the second international conference on Distributed event-based systems, pp. 35–46. ACM Press, New York (2008)
10. (SPARQL) SPARQL Query Language for RDF, W3C Recommendation (2008)

Decentralized Aggregation Protocols in Peer-to-Peer Networks: A Survey

Rafik Makhloufi, Grégory Bonnet, Guillaume Doyen, and Dominique Gaïti

ICD/ERA, FRE CNRS 2848, Université de Technologie de Troyes, 12 rue Marie
Curie, 10010 Troyes Cedex, France
{rafik.makhloufi,gregory.bonnet,guillaume.doyen,dominique.gaiti}@utt.fr

Abstract. In large scale decentralized and dynamic networks such as
Peer-to-Peer ones, being able to deal with quality of service requires the
establishment of a decentralized, autonomous and efficient management
strategy. In this context, there is a need to know the global state of
a network by collecting a variety of distributed statistical summary information through the use of aggregation protocols. In this paper, we
carried out a study on a set of aggregation protocols that can be used
for autonomous network monitoring purposes in P2P networks, and we
propose a classification and a comparison of them.

Keywords: aggregation protocols, Peer-to-Peer decentralized monitoring, gossip-based protocols, tree-based protocols.

1 Introduction

Size, complexity and user requirements in existing networks are constantly increasing, making current static and centralized management frameworks un-
adapted. Peer-to-Peer (P2P) networks are a good example of such networks since
they are known as large scale and dynamic ones, where resources are distributed
over the peers. This context involves the use of new decentralized and autonomic
management approaches in order to ensure some level of performance and QoS.
To reach this goal, a variety of statistical summary data about the network must
be collected in order to infer global information about the system. These distributed numeric values are collected by the aggregation protocols. Aggregation
is intended as a summarizing mechanism of the overall state within the network [25]. It refers to a set of functions that produce an indicator to evaluate a
global property of a system [20]. The summary data are obtained through the use
of a set of functions named aggregate functions. According to [26], there are basic aggregate functions: counts, sums, averages, minima and maxima, and over
these simple aggregates, more advanced aggregates can be computed such as:
histograms [13], parameter estimations [24,30], spectral analysis [16] or random
linear projections [23]. Another classification of the aggregate functions is done
in [18] according to other properties (e.g. duplicate sensitivity and monotony).

In this paper, we carry out a study of some of the aggregation protocols. We
propose a new classification followed by the description of these protocols in
Section 2 and we compare previously investigated protocols in Section 3 .

J.C. Strassner and Y.M. Ghamri-Doudane (Eds.): MACE 2009, LNCS 5844, pp. 111–116, 2009.

2   Taxonomy of Aggregation Protocols

Several aggregation protocols are proposed in large scale and dynamic networks such as grids, P2P, MANETs or sensor networks. In this paper, we focus our study on those that can be applied in a P2P context. Aggregation protocols are often classified in two prevailing categories: gossip-based protocols and tree-based protocols. Nonetheless, considering only these categories hides a lot of features and differences. Thus, we propose to refine this basic classification by introducing the following criteria, as shown in Figure 1.

1. **Network structure:** according to the degree of network structure, aggregation protocols can be classified into three categories: tree-based, gossip-based and hybrid protocols. Unlike tree-based techniques where nodes are organized into a tree, gossip-based protocols do not require a particular structure [5,10,14]. Computation of aggregates in tree-based techniques is often done hierarchically in a bottom-up fashion [3,9,17]. Finally, hybrid protocols combine a gossip dissemination mechanism with a tree structure.
2. **Propagation technique:** two way exist in which a node can exchange information with its neighbors: reactive and proactive[1] propagation techniques. Nodes use a reactive approach to reply by processing the query when a sender explicitly requests to compute an aggregate. A node uses the proactive approach to compute aggregates without explicitly asking for them (e.g. at each time interval or when changes occur) [12,19].
3. **Network view:** aggregates contain information about the global state of a network, but they may be computed across nodes in a neighborhood, a network domain or the entire network. Then, a node may have a situated view, limited to the neighborhood or a part of the network, or may have a global view about the entire network [8]. In our classification, a protocol has a situated view when it uses an explicit parameter that can be adjusted in order to have a view about some nodes or all the network nodes.
4. **Neighborhood information:** communication between nodes can be blind or informed. In blind communication, nodes do not hold information about other nodes. Thus a node selects neighbors to exchange information uniformly at random. By contrast, informed communication methods use heuristics for node selection (i.e. a non-uniform probabilistic distribution) [19].

2.1   Gossip-Based Aggregation Schemes

In each round of the basic gossip algorithms [7], a random pair of neighboring nodes is chosen to exchange their information. According to [26], gossip-based protocols can be divided regarding node selection into uniform gossip and standard gossip protocols. In uniform gossip, each node chooses to exchange information with a uniformly chosen node [14]. In standard gossip, neighbors are chosen according to a non-uniform probabilistic distribution [15,24]. Kempe et al. [14]

---

[1] Reactive and proactive methods are also called, respectively, pull and push methods.

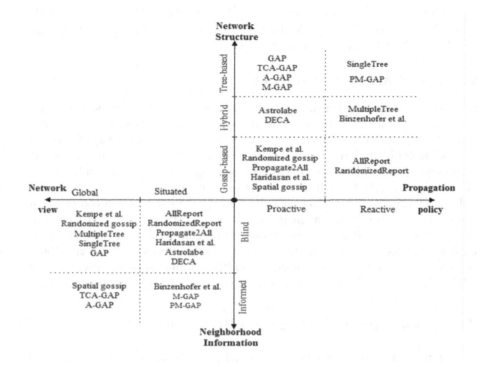

Fig. 1. Taxonomy of aggregation protocols in a P2P network

propose some uniform aggregation algorithms (e.g. the proactive blind `Push-sum` algorithm with a global view). Moreover, Bawa et al. [3] propose `Propagate2All` that enables a situated view by using a diameter D that denotes the upper bound to which the network is known, and they also present some reactive protocols: `AllReport` and `RandomizedReport` where a node replies with probability p. In the same category as `Propagate2All`, Haridasan et al. [11] propose an estimation-based protocol using data synopsis techniques [1]. An informed aggregation protocol named `Spatial gossip` is proposed in [15,24] where node selection is done according to the distance between the nodes.

2.2 Tree-Based Aggregation Schemes

Tree-based protocols use a tree for computing aggregates in a bottom-up fashion. The most basic protocol in this category is the blind reactive global view algorithm `SingleTree` [3], where a node q broadcasts a query to construct a spanning tree on the network. Dam and Stadler [9] propose a proactive protocol named GAP (Generic Aggregation Protocol) that builds and maintains a BFS spanning tree on the overlay network and uses it to incrementally and continuously compute and propagate aggregates. Improvements made on GAP gave form to several other protocols: a situated view and informed M-GAP where aggregates are available at all nodes, a reactive version of M-GAP named PM-GAP [29], TCA-GAP [28] for the decentralized detection of threshold crossings, A-GAP [21,22] an adaptive extension of GAP.

2.3 Hybrid Aggregation Schemes

In order to combine the benefits of both gossip and tree, some protocols propose an hybrid approach that uses a gossip dissemination over a tree structure. Bawa et al. [3] propose the reactive blind situated view algorithm `MultipleTree`, an enhancement of `SingleTree` that creates k independent spanning trees rooted at the querying node. Moreover, others propose to organize nodes into a hierarchy of a maximal height h) with a situated view. For exemple, `Astrolabe` [6,25] is a distributed information management system that uses gossip to construct an overlay tree for computing aggregates. For structured networks, Artigas et al. propose the use of `DECA` [2], where nodes are organized into clusters and super-clusters. In this same context, Binzenhofer et al. [4] propose an informed and reactive approach that uses a snapshot algorithm at an arbitrary peer of a Chord DHT [27] to divide recursively the overlay into contiguous subparts of size c.

3   Comparison of Aggregation Protocols

We carry out a comparison of some aggregation protocols seen above according to the following evaluation criteria: (1) the computation cost for a protocol is the maximum computation cost among all the nodes in the network, and for a single node the computation cost is the number of steps taken by the process that is executed on the node; (2) the communication cost is the sum of sizes of messages sent between any node pairs during aggregation; (3) the robustness that defines the capacity of a system to operate correctly and to ensure accuracy despite of external factors such as node or link failures; (4) the convergence time that is the necessary time between the initialization of the aggregation and the time when all nodes (or querying node) hold the aggregation results (i.e. the elapsed time for both communication and computation).

The collected comparison results presented in Table 1 obtained from the literature show that gossip-based protocols ensure fault-tolerance due to their decentralization, and also provide a better convergence time due to the gossip diffusion speed. However, the large number of exchanged messages causes more overhead and a high communication and computation cost. Tree-based protocols execute themselves in a better convergence time and a lower communication and computation cost due to their optimization of the number of exchanged messages on the tree. However, the hierarchical structure and the unique path between each node and the root let tree-based protocols be more sensitive to faults than the decentralized gossip-based protocols. Hybrid protocols combine the benefits of the two approaches. So, they are more resilient than tree-based protocols and they have less overhead than gossip-based protocols.

Table 1. Comparison of aggregation protocols

		Communication cost	Computation cost	Convergence time	Robustness
Gossip	Kempe et al.	$O(n \log n)$	$O(\log n)$	$O(\log n)$	√
	Propagate2All	$O(mnr)$	$O(n)$	$O(\hat{D})$	√
	AllReport	$O(m+n)$	$O(n)$	NA	√
	Randomized-Report	$O(m+np)$	$O(n)$	NA	√
	Spatial gossip	$O(\sqrt{n})$	$O(n \log n)$	$O(n^{3/2} \log n)$	√
Tree	SingleTree	$O(m+nr)$	$O(b)$	$O(D)$	×
	GAP	$1.7 msg/sec/node*$	NA	$1.5-3sec*$	×
	A-GAP	NA	$< 0.5 sec/node*$	$< 4ms*$	√
	TCA-GAP	$\simeq GAP*$	NA	$0.5-1.75sec*$	×
Hybrid	Multiple-Tree	$O(m+knr)$	$O(k+b)$	$O(D)$	√
	Astrolabe	$\simeq 1msg/round/node*$	$O(\log n)$	NA	√
	DECA	$O(logn)$	$O(rn \log n + rn)$	$O(\log c + h)$	√

√: supported; ×: not supported; NA: not available; *: depends on experiments.

4 Conclusion and Future Work

In this paper, we handle the problem of decentralized monitoring and computing aggregates in P2P networks. We examine and classify a set of aggregation protocols for P2P networks. We also address a comparison of these protocols. The aggregation protocol has to be simple, scalable and ensures robustness, convergence time and low communication and computation cost. Despite the amount of work carried out towards the development of efficient aggregation protocols, there is no protocol that guarantees all the desired performance criteria at the same time. Gossip-based protocols are generally simple, scalable and more resilient to faults, but they cause a high communication and computation cost while tree-based protocols cause a lower communication cost with sensitivity to faults. We plan to extend our work by consolidating the comparison of aggregation protocols with more performance criteria and quantitative results.

References

1. Aggarwal, C.C., Yu, P.S.: A survey of synopsis construction in data streams. In: Data streams: models and algorithms. Springer, Heidelberg (2006)
2. Artigas, M.S., López, P.G., Gómez-Skarmeta, A.F.: DECA: a hierarchical framework for decentralized aggregation in DHTs. In: State, R., van der Meer, S., O'Sullivan, D., Pfeifer, T. (eds.) DSOM 2006. LNCS, vol. 4269, pp. 246–257. Springer, Heidelberg (2006)
3. Bawa, M., Garcia-Molina, H., Gionis, A., Motwani, R.: Estimating aggregates on a peer-to-peer network. Tech. rep., Stanford InfoLab (2003)
4. Binzenhofer, A., Kunzmann, G., Henjes, R.: A scalable algorithm to monitor chord-based p2p systems at runtime. In: Proc. IPDPS (2006)
5. Birman, K.: The promise, and limitations, of gossip protocols. SIGOPS Oper. Syst. Rev. 41(5), 8–13 (2007)
6. Birman, K., van Renesse, R., Vogels, W.: Scalable data fusion using astrolabe. In: Proc. FUSION (2002)

7. Boyd, S., Ghosh, A., Prabhakar, B., Shah, D.: Randomized gossip algorithms. IEEE/ACM Trans. Netw. 14, SI, 2508–2530 (2006)
8. Bullot, T., Khatoun, R., Hugues, L., Gaïti, D., Merghem-Boulahia, L.: A situatedness-based knowledge plane for autonomic networking. Int. J. Netw. Manag. 18(2), 171–193 (2008)
9. Dam, M., Stadler, R.: A generic protocol for network state aggregation. In: Proc. RVK (2005)
10. Dietzfelbinger, M.: Gossiping and broadcasting versus computing functions in networks. Discrete Appl. Math. 137(2), 127–153 (2004)
11. Haridasan, M., van Renesse, R.: Gossip-based distribution estimation in peer-to-peer networks. In: Proc. IPTPS (2008)
12. Jelasity, M., Montresor, A., Babaoglu, O.: Gossip-based aggregation in large dynamic networks. ACM Trans. Comput. Syst. 23(3), 219–252 (2005)
13. Jurca, D., Stadler, R.: Computing histograms of local variables for real-time monitoring using aggregation trees. In: Proc. IM (2009)
14. Kempe, D., Dobra, A., Gehrke, J.: Gossip-based computation of aggregate information. In: Proc. FOCS (2003)
15. Kempe, D., Kleinberg, J., Demers, A.: Spatial gossip and resource location protocols. In: Proc. STOC (2001)
16. Kempe, D., McSherry, F.: A decentralized algorithm for spectral analysis. In: Proc. STOC (2004)
17. Li, J., yoh Lim, D.: A robust aggregation tree on distributed hash tables. In: Proc. MIT SOW (2004)
18. Madden, S., Franklin, M.J., Hellerstein, J.M., Hong, W.: TAG: a tiny aggregation service for ad-hoc sensor networks. SIGOPS Oper. Syst. Rev. 36, SI, 131–146 (2002)
19. Meshkovaa, E., Riihijärvia, J., Petrovaa, M., Mähönen, P.: A survey on resource discovery mechanisms, peer-to-peer and service discovery frameworks. Computer Networks 52(11), 2097–2128 (2008)
20. Montresor, A., Jelasity, M., Babaoglu, O.: Robust aggregation protocols for large-scale overlay networks. In: Proc. DSN (2004)
21. Prieto, A.G., Stadler, R.: Adaptive distributed monitoring with accuracy objectives. In: Proc. INM (2006)
22. Prieto, A.G., Stadler, R.: A-GAP: an adaptive protocol for continuous network monitoring with accuracy objectives. IEEE TNSM 4(1), 2–12 (2007)
23. Rabbat, M., Haupt, J., Singh, A., Nowak, R.: Decentralized compression and predistribution via randomized gossiping. In: Proc. IPSN (2006)
24. Rabbat, M.G.: On spatial gossip algorithms for average consensus. In: Proc. SSP (2007)
25. Renesse, R.V., Birman, K.P., Vogels, W.: Astrolabe: a robust and scalable technology for distributed system monitoring, management, and data mining. ACM Trans. Comput. Syst. 21(2), 164–206 (2003)
26. Sarkar, R., Zhu, X., Gao, J.: Hierarchical spatial gossip for multi-resolution representations in sensor networks. In: Proc. IPSN (2007)
27. Stoica, I., Morris, R., Karger, D., Kaashoek, M.F., Balakrishnan, H.: Chord: a scalable peer-to-peer lookup service for internet applications. In: Proc. SIGCOMM (2001)
28. Wuhib, F., Dam, M., Stadler, R.: Decentralized detection of global threshold crossings using aggregation trees. Computer Networks 52(9), 1745–1761 (2008)
29. Wuhib, F., Stadler, R.: M-GAP: a new pattern for cfengine and other distributed software. Tech. rep., Royal Institute of Technology, KTH (2008)
30. Xiao, L., Boyd, S., Lall, S.: A scheme for robust distributed sensor fusion based on average consensus. In: Proc. IPSN (2005)

Author Index